Praise for An Upward Calling:

"Michael Stafford's essays are eloquent, insightful commentaries on the stewardship ethic of traditional conservatism. His book is a refreshing counter-narrative to the bombastic egotism and impious lack of restraint that masquerades as conservatism today."
- Jim DiPeso, Republicans for Environmental Protection

"Instead of attacking what conservatism is not, An Upward Calling affirms what conservatism is by tracing its legacy and suggesting its future in crisp, inventive language that engenders trust, and inspires deeper study."
- Eric Byler, Coffee Party USA

"Michael's is a voice that needs to be heard in American politics, a voice that respectfully and soundly calls for common sense, decency, and real plans of action for our society. This is a must read for anyone who is interested in becoming a more engaged member of society."
- Ken Grant, former Communications Director of the Delaware Republican Party

"Writing in the elevating, enlightening tradition of great Catholic thinkers like Moynihan, Buckley, Novak and Weigel, Stafford lays a new marker down for the next generation of patriotic, public service-minded faithful, challenging us all to be true to the 'Upward Calling' that we are born to aspire. His call for a compassionate, socially responsible, conservatism is particularly needed in our nation today."
- Michael Fleming, former Delaware Republican Party officer

AN UPWARD CALLING

POLITICS FOR THE COMMON GOOD

BY MICHAEL STAFFORD

AVTBooks

Bringing Words To Life In A Digital World

An Upward Calling: Politics for the Common Good
By Michael Stafford

Published by AVT Books, Milton, Delaware
www.avtbooks.com

ISBN-13: 978-0-9836804-0-6

The cover photo is of the window "Education" at Yale, taken by Sage Ross, from commons.wikimedia.org and is reprinted with permission.

Table of Contents

Introduction

Almost three years ago, reading "*Render unto Caesar: Serving the Nation by Living our Catholic Beliefs in Political Life*" by the Most Reverend Charles J. Chaput, O.F.M. Cap., Archbishop of Denver, inspired me to take an active leadership role in the Delaware Republican Party. I certainly picked an interesting time to get involved. In his book, Archbishop Chaput noted that neither political party provides a comfortable home for Roman Catholics. My experiences, which are the genesis of this book, have been a testament to the truth of that statement.

Originally, each chapter was written as a separate, stand-alone essay. They can still be read as such. However, they share common themes that tie them into a cohesive whole. Taken together, they constitute an invitation to something better in the public life and politics of our society. This is critical today. The economic blows of the past several years have been extremely unsettling. Americans seem to have lost a great deal of their former hope and optimism, as well as their faith in each other. More broadly, there is a widely shared perception that *something* is terribly amiss in our country - socially, politically, and economically. This book is an (admittedly small) attempt to mark a path towards a better common future for us all and to restore faith in the notion that our tomorrow will be better then our today.

Obviously, given the foregoing, this is in some ways a very

Catholic book, written from the perspective of a dissident conservative active in Republican politics at a time when the political Right is becoming increasingly radicalized. Themes prevalent in Catholic social doctrine, such as subsidiarity, solidarity, stewardship, and human dignity, inform much of the writing. And the essays speak directly to the need for a limited but vigorous government capable of serving the common good by advancing social, economic, and environmental justice. The book also draws heavily on the work of America's greatest Catholic conservative thinker, Russell Kirk. And, in some cases, the essays are directly addressed to contemporary Republicans. Still, I hope the material is presented in a way that is accessible, acceptable, and meaningful to all people of good will, of whatever faith or political persuasion.

If this book leads anyone to a deeper exploration of Russell Kirk's writings, then it will have largely served its purpose. Brad Bizer has described Russell Kirk as a "Knight-Errant against the ideologues."[1] At a time when conservatives are busy setting up Test Acts and purity tests, Kirk reminds us that conservatism used to be a broad, intellectually vibrant hall whose boundaries were not definitively marked by fixed points of ideology or doctrine. At the same time, his vision of a conservatism with a social conscience is desperately needed today, given the rise of extreme ideological libertarianism.

Kirk's struggle against the totalitarians and ideologues is one we must take up with renewed vigor and fortitude. Goodness, truth, and decency require public referents. A world overrun by zealots of every conceivable political and theological stripe requires rallying points. It needs places where a standard has been planted that people of good will can gather around.

This book is an attempt to plant one such standard and I hope it inspires you to join in "the good fight on the darkling plain."[2]   I think our future depends upon it.

The act of creation is always a labor of love. This is especially true in the realm of ideas. We each, with our words and our actions, stand upon the shore of a great lake, figuratively casting in stones -- stones for good, and stones for ill. From each impact, ripples radiate out across the surface of the water. Where they will go, and whom they will touch is not given us to know.

It is an act of faith.

--

[1] Bizer, Brad. (Mar. 11, 2011). "Russell Kirk: Knight-Errant Against the Ideologues." The Imaginative Conservative. Retrieved from: http://www.imaginativeconservative.org/2010/09/ russell-kirk-knight-errant-against.html

[2] Id.

1.

The Seriousness of the Moment: Holding the Center

Pope John Paul II once said "[M]an always travels along precipices. His truest obligation is to keep his balance."[3]

This is certainly correct - much of human history consists of civilization, figuratively, careening from one crisis to another. Each generation, of course, is apt to think that its own particular problems are a decisive turning point on which the fate of the world hangs. Perhaps it is natural that we succumb to such conceits, that we fancy a special place and significance for our own time in history.

At the risk of falling prey to the very conceit I have warned of above, converging arguments have persuaded me that we are living at a decisive moment in human history - *a tipping point.*

Today, America, and the world, are at a critical crossroads.

We are encompassed by many perils - a range of complex and seemingly intractable problems. They include the recession, the disappearance of manufacturing sector jobs, the growth of income inequality, the ballooning federal budget deficit, the rising cost and depersonalization of health care, environmental degradation and global warming, the quickening pace of technological change, the proliferation of weapons of mass destruction, and the rise of foreign powers fundamentally hostile to liberty and freedom.

Collectively, these problems are best seen as dangerous vectors coursing through modernity.

Moreover, we face these fiscal, economic, environmental, and international challenges at a time of profound social and demographic change at home. America is growing more ethnically and racially diverse while it is simultaneously growing older. The inevitable movement towards being a "majority minority" nation and the aging of our population produce a range of fears and social stresses that are amplified and exacerbated by fiscal and economic ones.

Furthermore, we are facing these challenges and changes at a time when our political discourse is fundamentally poisoned. As one author has observed, "[o]ur sense of civic togetherness has taken a beating since the 2000 election" which has been followed by a burst (initially by the Left, and now, following President Obama's election, by the Right) "of almost pathological anxiety, social alienation, partisan cynicism, and civic despair."[4]

Simply put, a level of unease and anxiety abounds in the land that is unprecedented in our recent history. Given the nature and magnitude of the challenges we are facing, a high level of concern is warranted.

The point of our labor then is to make certain that our future world will be a decent one - one in which human dignity will be respected, and in which human liberty will flourish. This ought to be the common object of all people of good will.

Unfortunately, times of great social stress and anxiety create opportunities for demagogues - "panic peddlers" - who are willing to pander to people's fears, willing to offer scapegoats, willing to provide simplistic explanations and solutions.

We can find solutions to the problems facing us, but only if we stand in solidarity with one another. We have no hope if we are at each other's throats. For this reason, we must reject the politics and rhetoric of fear, anger, and resentment that have so poisoned our public discourse on both the Left and the Right, and embrace the politics of love. Love is our only hope.

Love requires solidarity - a recognition that we are all equals, and that we bear a responsibility both for each other and for advancing the common good. Solidarity is the antidote to our toxic public discourse because it invites us to see "the other" for what they truly are - not some malevolent figure, not an enemy, but our brother, our sister. "The other" is not a stranger, but rather a reflection of you - a being of immeasurable dignity. And when there is no "other" on which to pin our fears or our anger, then the politics of resentment falls away into nothing.

Love is our only hope. If we remember this, then, together, we can turn our challenges into opportunities, our perils into the promise of a better and more just future for us all. But time presses; there will come a point beyond which it will be too late to act, beyond which our options narrow, and become far more limited.

Atlas wearies of his burden

We live at a time when the hegemonic power of America appears to be waning, particularly in the economic realm. As Peggy Noonan has repeatedly noted, we have lived through "the great abundance" and it is, at best, unclear when and if we shall see the like of it again.[5]

This is significant. America is the Atlas that has held up the world's material prosperity and physical security. For better, or worse, we are the Leviathan- the power that makes the rules and enforces order, in the international system. And despite whatever unfairness there is in it, America's global stewardship - *Pax Americana* - has coincided with an age of unprecedented prosperity in which millions of people have been lifted out of abject poverty around the world and into an emergent global middle class.

But Atlas also bears a second burden. The cause of human liberty and freedom is inextricably intertwined with the fate of our nation.

When England's power waned in the middle of the last century, she had a rising United States that, fundamentally, shared her values to whom she could pass the baton of world leadership. We have no such friendly entity, no such sympathetic power, on the horizon today. Talk of an emerging multipolar world seems innocuous enough, until one stops to consider that many of the rising powers within it - think Iran here - are fundamentally hostile both to our interests and to the cause of liberty.

At the dawn of this century, we saw, on a bright September morning, that bandits living in caves in the remote corners of the world possess the ability to wreak havoc in the continental United States on a scale beyond the capability of Nazi Germany or Imperial Japan at the height of their powers. No ocean, no mere geographical separation or physical barrier, can provide security in the future.

The end of the *Pax Romana* ushered in the Dark Ages - a time when life was nasty, brutish, and short. A time when, at least in Western Europe, the fire of civilization flickered and threatened to go out. What will the end of the *Pax Americana*, if it comes, mean to peace, stability, and human rights?

Mortgaging the future (in more ways that one)

At the same time, our Federal government has embarked on an unprecedented spending spree while, simultaneously, refusing to raise the necessary revenues, or make the required programmatic cuts and changes, to deal with structural issues in the federal budget, such as rising healthcare costs, that are driving us into insolvency. As a direct result, our national debt is rising to an unprecedented level.[6] America didn't become a hegemonic power by exporting its public debts to the world, and we're unlikely to remain one for very long if this situation persists.

Our deficit spending constitutes an enormous intergenerational transfer of wealth - we are quite literally mortgaging our children's future.[7] At the same time, we are substantially restricting our own scope of future action.

Our refusal to look at both sides of the budget equation - the relationship between revenues and expenditures, coupled with exploding healthcare costs and an aging population, has put us on an unsustainable trajectory. Simply put, "[w]ithin the next decade, nondiscretionary programs including Social Security and Medicare and interest on the national debt will consume 90 cents of every federal tax dollar. That leaves a dime of every dollar left for every other priority, including defense, education and homeland security."[8] These are systemic problems that will not become more soluble with the mere passage of time.

We tend to assume that the way things are today was somehow predetermined or preordained, rather then being what it is - the contingent outcome of choices made by past generations. As those with living memories of the Depression pass from the scene, they leave a country in which everyone has come of age in a world dominated, both economically and militarily, by America. A world in which our power and preeminence is presumed. In which one generation always does better then the next. In which entry into the meritocracy of good paying professional jobs is open to anyone with some brains and a bit of drive and ambition. And it is hard for many people to imagine a world in which those comfortable presumptions no longer hold true.

That world though, if we are not careful, lurks right around the corner.

Childhood's End

Serious times and issues demand a certain modicum of maturity from those who purport to care about the fate of the world.

So, in the words the late Pope John Paul II, I appeal to you to be "convinced of the seriousness of the moment, to fulfill your commitment [to the common good] by the way you live, by the use of your resources, by your civic activity, by contributing to economic and political decisions, and by personal involvement in national and international undertakings."[9]

If we want a future in which our children and grandchildren are able to reach their full potential, then *the time to act is now*. Ensuring that the precipice is navigated safely is the life's work of all people of good will.

It is incumbent upon us to show that the best still have conviction. Together, we can avoid the dystopian futures threatening on the horizon, and bequeath to the next generation an opportunity. And that, perhaps, is all that loving parents can ever do.

--

[3] Retrieved from: http://en.wikiquote.org/wiki/Talk:Pope_John_Paul_II

[4] Bauer, Fred. (May 25, 2010). "How to Build a better GOP." FrumForum. Retrieved from: http://www.frumforum.com/how-to-build-a-better-gop

[5] Noonan, Peggy. (Mar. 12, 2009). "There's No Pill for This Kind of Depression." The Wall Street Journal.

[6] Hinderaker, John. (Feb. 1, 2010). "Obama Parts Company With Reality." Power Line. Retrieved from: http://www.powerlineblog.com/archives/ 2010/02/025508.php

[7] Haque, Umair. (Jan. 27, 2010). "Obama's Budget Freeze and America's Economic Decline." Harvard Business Review (blog).

[8] Watts, J.C. (Mar. 20, 2011). "A Staggering Absence of Leadership." Las Vegas Review-Journal.

[9] Pope John Paul II. (Dec. 30, 1987). On Social Concern (Solicitudo Rei Socialis). Papal Archive. The Holy See.

2.

Living Together

"How ought we to live together?" With those words, Aristotle framed the fundamental question at the heart of politics in a democratic society.

How, indeed? Notice that word "ought." It implies something more than mere choices from a range of neutral, equivalent possibilities. It implies a gradation from worse to better. It implies the existence of an ideal form towards which we should be moving.

Let me propose an answer to this question that might serve as a guidepost for all of us, Republican or Democrat, Conservative or Liberal, as we navigate the public arena.

We live in an era marked by incivility. We speak of a country divided between red states and blue states, between conservatives and liberals, and these are very real, substantive, divisions. However, there is another, unmentioned, division that is more fundamental which blurs these boundaries.

How ought we to live together? The answer is simple: with love.

Love is not a word one hears frequently in conservative circles. It conjures images of hippies wearing tie-dyed t-shirts and playing tambourines, not the Conservative Political Action Conference. That is a shame. Russell Kirk, for example, recognized that:

> "[a]t the back of every discussion of the good society lies this question, What is the object of human life? The enlightened conservative does not believe that the end or aim of life is competition; or success; or enjoyment; or longevity; or power; or possessions. He believes, instead, that the object of life is Love."[10]

Love, *agape*, forms the sole foundation, the essential predicate, to serving the common good.

Humanity divides into those who see "the other" as an erring brother (or sister, as the case may be), and those who see enemies and evil monsters; between those who are motivated by love, and those who are driven by anger and fear. Love is the ultimate constructive force in human history; hatred always leads to one destination - ruin.

I'm not naïve - our political discourse has always been marked, at times, by a certain level of bitterness and incivility. It commenced almost at the very beginning. Philip Freneau's heated polemics in the *National Gazette*, for example, would make even the most zealous radio talk show host, blogger, or MoveOn.org activist blush.

Human nature being what it is, this style of public discourse will always be with us.

So, why do I bother climbing up on the soap box to declaim what simply is? It's a legitimate question. The answer is rooted in one significant word: "ought."

What does it mean to say that we "ought" to live together with love? It does not mean that we will agree on the means, or on specific policies - people of good will routinely disagree about how best to achieve the common good. There will never be a consensus and we might even disagree at times about what the "common good" is. Rather, it speaks more to the way we disagree, and how we view each other across the chasm of the partisan divide.

I was appalled at the language used by many on the far left during the Bush years. The analogies to the tyrants of the mid twentieth century- analogies which profane both the true horror that those tyrants represent, and the loss suffered by so many millions at their hands. I was appalled at the mockery, the constant effort to strip away legitimacy, the endless conspiracy theories, and the ever-present willingness to believe that those on the other side of the political divide are- mostly- evil and capable of anything.[11]

And now, Bush having passed from the scene, we see similar behavior by many on the right. Again, we have the offensive analogies and artwork comparing President Obama (and others) to various totalitarian figures. We have the insanity of the Birther conspiracy theories. We have the immediate rush to delegitimize.

The common denominator in much of this is the absence of love. Reduce the other side to a tag word, a code phrase, and you no longer need to pay much attention to what they actually have to say. Append an epithet, demonize them, and your opponents cease, for practical purposes, to even be human beings. Relationships among equals should be governed by mutual respect, but this is impossible in such a hostile, tribal climate of fear and suspicion.

I think the rhetoric in the 2012 elections will be more harsh and divisive than ever before (on both sides). We must recognize - it is not *my* country, it is not *your* country: it is *our* country. In the end, we are all in this together.

The present state of our public discourse, and the irresponsible behavior of the extremists on both the Left and the Right, calls to mind Abraham Lincoln's letter to Major General Joseph Hooker in January, 1863:[12]

> "I much fear that the spirit which you have aided to infuse into the army, of criticizing their commander and withholding confidence from him, will now turn upon you. I shall assist you as far as I can to put it down. Neither you nor Napoleon, if he were alive again, could get any good out of an army while such a spirit prevails in it."

Today, what fell "spirit" have we infused into the public life of our nation? And, what leader, from either political party, will be able to get any good out of our country "while such a spirit prevails"?

We'd do well not to further poison our public well.

--

[10] Kirk, R. (1989). Prospects for Conservatives. (Washington,

D.C.: Regnery), 21.

[11] In retrospect, it appears clear that the rhetoric and conspiracy theories directed at Bill and Hillary Clinton during the 1990's by the Republican opposition, as well as the investigations and the impeachment process, was extremely reckless and played a key role in setting this process in motion. In many ways, it began the process of poisoning our public discourse. In the manner of our opposition, we (meaning conservatives and the GOP) did great and lasting damage to the legitimacy of our government and our institutions. The legal wrangling in *Bush v. Gore*, brought on by Vice President Al Gore's reckless decision to challenge the legitimacy of the outcome of the 2000 Presidential election, simply further exacerbated matters and amplified the damage.

[12] Retrieved from: http://www.civil-war.net/pages/ general_hooker_letter.asp

3.

Moral Strategy: The Case For Pragmatic Conservatism

Idealism and realism are in constant tension. From a political perspective, it is necessary for conservatives to strike a balance between the two. Standing alone, realism all too often shades into cynicism, idealism into flights of utopian fancy. In the end, however, we must see the world as it is in order to shape the world as we imagine it ought to be.

In the GOP today, the dialectic between realism and idealism manifests itself both in the debate over the support given to more centrist candidates and in the proposals to adopt various litmus or purity tests. Specifically, this debate often involves arguments in which one side focuses on electability, while the other focuses almost exclusively on ideological purity.

Frankly, both sides miss the mark. The GOP exists both to win elections and to "advance substantive ideas and public policies."[13] The key is to strike an appropriate balance, candidate by candidate, race by race, between the two.

We live at a moment in history pregnant with both great opportunity and with tremendous peril. There is a great deal of unease, of disquiet, of fear abroad in the land. What our future world will look like is still inchoate. The point of our labors then, is to make certain that this future world will be a decent one - one in which human dignity will be respected, in which human liberty will flourish, and in which the wolf will be kept away from the door.

Now is the time for moral strategy - for an intellectually serious, pragmatic, tactically savvy, conservatism devoid of demagoguery and utopian dreams of unattainable ideological purity - one capable of building and sustaining a diverse center-right electoral coalition far into the future.

Thankfully, we have signposts in our past to guide us in the present.

Pointing the way ahead: Lincoln

Lincoln is, in my view, the ultimate example of a "moral strategist" in American political history. The moral issue he faced, of course, was the abolition of slavery. Living in a profoundly racist society, and in the midst of a civil war calling into doubt the future existence of the nation he governed, Lincoln adroitly maneuvered to bring an end to that most awful institution. In doing so, he moved cautiously, pragmatically, realistically appraising the scope of what was politically possible at every step. Throughout the Civil War, he held together a diverse coalition of Radical Republicans and other, less ideologically committed elements. In the 1850's, abolition was a utopian dream; by the 1860's, it was reality. Nothing better demonstrates what can be accomplished through moral strategy.

A considerable diversity of opinion

In addition to Lincoln's example, calls for purity, litmus tests and the purging of those deemed ideologically suspect from the ranks of the GOP are a departure from traditional conservatism. They are also, from a practical perspective, rather short sighted & self-destructive.

Historically, according to Russell Kirk:[14]

> "Being neither a religion nor an ideology, the body of opinion termed conservatism possesses no Holy Writ and no Das Kapital to provide dogmata... The attitude we call conservatism is sustained by a body of sentiments, rather than by a system of ideological dogmata. ... The conservative movement or body of opinion can accommodate a considerable diversity of views on a good many subjects, there being no Test Act or Thirty-Nine Articles of the conservative creed."

Moreover, as Michael Powell has observed, a fixation on ideological purity and litmus tests inhibits the development of new ideas because "[t]he formation of powerful ideas requires the push and pull of varying viewpoints testing and informing one another."[15]

From a practical standpoint, Ronald Reagan understood the imperative to build a broad, diverse electoral coalition. He assiduously avoided litmus-test politics. It's not a coincidence that he is remembered as one of our greatest Presidents, and there is immense irony in the effort to co-opt his "unity principle" in support of the efforts to develop new purity tests for the GOP.

A path forward

The challenges we face as a people are extremely serious. Politics is not a game devoid of consequences.

We need new moral strategists, leaders capable of striking the right balance between realism and idealism, of working pragmatically to build coalitions. After all, "conciliation while maintaining core principles is not only possible, but it also provides the most likely path to victory."[16]

Let's put away childish things, like quests for ideological purity, blind dogmatism, or support for fringe, demonstrably unelectable, figures. Make no mistake, we have an enormous task ahead.

--

[13] Guardiano, John. (Jan. 4, 2010). "Bring on the GOP Slugfest." FrumForum. Retrieved from: http://www.frumforum.com/bring-on-the-gop-slugfest

[14] Kirk, Russell. (1993). "Ten Conservative Principles." The Russell Kirk Center for Cultural Renewal. Retrieved from: http://www.klrk-center.org/index.php/detail/ten-conservative-principles/

[15] Powell, Michael K. (Jan. 19, 2009). "The Republican Party Is On The Precipice of Irrelevance." FrumForum. Retrieved from: http://www.frumforum.com/the-republican-party-is-on-the-precipice-of-irrelevance

[16] Marsico, Jennifer. (Jan. 20, 2010). "The GOP's Northeast Resurgence." FrumForum. Retrieved from: http://www.frumforum.com/the-gops-northeast-resurgence

4.

Communitarianism: A Renewed Focus on Civil Society & Civic Virtue

I am not a libertarian. My own political thought is based on the idea that liberty and duty, freedom and obligation, are always paired. I am constantly striving to achieve the right balance between them on any given issue. Perhaps this is why Burke's notion of the intergenerational contract resonates so deeply with me.

Human beings are not wholly autonomous sovereignties. Such a view presents an inauthentic, or at least, incomplete, conceptualization of our nature. And it is one that ultimately ends in anomie.

For these reasons, I am deeply troubled by the modern

emphasis - prevalent across the entirety of the ideological spectrum in our nation - on an individualism that exalts selfishness and short-term material gratification over broader commitments and concerns. America has seen the development of something that almost constitutes a new religion, the "Cult of Self."[17] It is a Cult that is sustained and nurtured by modern mass culture. And the rise of an extreme form of ideological libertarianism within the Republican Party is one of its political manifestations.

As Robert Locke noted in a 2005 essay in *The American Conservative*: "[i]f Marxism is the delusion that one can run society purely on altruism and collectivism, then libertarianism is the mirror-image delusion that one can run it purely on selfishness and individualism."[18]

Libertarianism is an organizational model more suited to an imagined society of essentially independent and self-sufficient yeoman farmers and frontiersmen then to a modern world composed primarily of more complexly organized urban and suburban communities. The foregoing is a very convoluted way of saying that libertarianism fails the moment your neighbors put up a ghastly pink flamingo in their front yard and you pick up the phone and complain to the community association.

In addition, libertarianism has two more subtle flaws. First, it neglects the fact that seemingly minor individual choices can, cumulatively, have a huge impact on society. Second, carried to its logical conclusion, it rejects any positive role for government in creating or sustaining the social and economic conditions necessary for the full development of the human person - including things such as ensuring access to adequate health-care, providing for an equitable distribution of wealth and opportunity, addressing global environmental concerns, and the problems of conservation and stewardship. This latter point, I think, often comes across as a lack of compassion or empathy for others (from a public policy standpoint); or, put a different way, in a focus on the impact of government policy on "me" rather then on society as a whole. This is evident even in some of the terminology used in public policy debates: you will here people scream about how the government utilizes "my" tax dollars when, really, it's about the use of "our" taxes.

Unfortunately, radical libertarians are gaining strength is today's Republican Party and in the broader conservative movement. In so doing, they are crowding out traditional, more socially responsible, visions of political conservatism. As David Jenkins of Republicans for Environmental Protection has observed:[19]

> "The Republican Party has been hijacked. I maintain that it is being unduly influenced by what I call 'pretend conservatives.' These are the radical libertarians that dominate right-wing talk radio and outlets like Fox News. If you listen to people like Rush Limbaugh and Glenn Beck you cannot really find any traditionalist conservative ideas in their world view.

> The policies being peddled by these folks reflect a *live for today - let me do what I want* mentality that has nothing to do with the conservative notion of protecting the interests of future generations. Their support for fiscal restraint is primarily due to their desire to starve and weaken the federal government, not to protect our children and grandchildren from debt. Otherwise, they should be able to recognize that fiscal stewardship and environmental stewardship are

equally conservative. Their energy and environmental views promote waste, pollution, and overdependence on finite resources. Is there anything less conservative than waste?

I personally would call them liberal, because their attitude reminds me of the liberal 'if it feels good do it' mantra of the 1960s, only the vices are different."

"Let me do what I want"- nothing better summarizes the myopic vision of the politics of the "Cult of Self."[20]

Thankfully, there is a different way to think about the relationship between the individual and society (and the state), a different way to conceive of the pairing of individual rights with public obligations - communitarianism. It offers a framework that serves as a better guide in striking the right balance between the competing claims of the individual and society - between selfishness and altruism- when crafting public policy.

As Oliver Garland has argued, this might be accomplished by reconciling "classical conservatism with an old (although until recently forgotten) philosophy of communitarianism into a new conservatism for the 21st century." Unlike traditional liberalism, communitarianism "does not view the individual as merely an isolated economic agent whose only association with society is free and voluntary." Instead, it recognizes that individuals are "shaped and formed by their societies and communities and that with their rights and liberties come great responsibilities and obligations."

As Garland correctly observes:

"Conservatives need to adopt a more proactive policy in helping people instead of just leaving them alone to the barren marketplace. This does not mean abandoning the market-oriented policies of conservatism but instead suggests that we temper the private sector and the public sector with the civil society sector. It is reminiscent of President Bush's compassionate conservatism but with a more expansive vision for the future of America…

This new fusionist philosophy can help solve many of society's problems and foster a more civic-minded approach that remembers that people are not born into isolation but are, as Aristotle says, 'political animals'." [21]

Fundamentally, communitarianism marks a decisive break with the Right's enthrallment to the unregulated, unrestricted, "free" market. It recognizes that "economic liberalism has often been a cover for monopoly capitalism and is therefore just as socially damaging as left-wing statism."[22]

Politically, communitarianism stands as a defense of society, of the common good, from both "the unrestrained free market and the unlimited state."[23] It can, in other words, provide a new alternative between rule by uncaring corporations and the bureaucratic centralized state. As Phillip Blond has noted (albeit, in the English political context), communitarian conservatism, "could reject the politics of class—of 'our people'—and the interests of the already wealthy in favour of a national politics that serves the needs of all."[24]

In the end, communitarianism comports with authentic human development. People, after all, are social beings. And, as Russell Kirk recognized, "[i]t is in community that human beings realize their aim in existence."[25]

--

[17] I'm not sure who, precisely, owns pride of authorship in the coining of this term. For my own part, I encountered it for the first time in Chris Hedge's writing.

[18] Locke, Robert. (Mar. 14, 2005). "Marxism of the Right." The American Conservative.

[19] Revkin, Andrew. (Mar. 14, 2011). "'Republicans for Environmental Protection'- Endangered Species?" The New York Times. Retrieved from: http://dotearth.blogs.nytimes.com/2011/03/14/republicans-for-environmental-protection-endangered-species/

[20] As an interesting aside, despite the presence of many self-described conservative Christians among the ranks of the radical libertarians, their political philosophy shares more in common with the Wiccan Rede than with the New Testament- "an it harm none, do what ye will."

[21] Garland, Oliver R. (April 19, 2010) "Getting Conservatives to Care About Community." FrumForum. Retrieved from: http://www.frumforum.com/whu-conservatives-should-care-about-community

[22] Blond, Phillip. (Feb. 28, 2009). "Rise of the Red Tories." Prospect, Issue 155.

[23] Id.

[24] Id.

[25] Kirk, R. (1991). The Roots of American Order, 3rd ed. (Washington, D.C.: Regnery), 89.

5.

"Green Elephants": Environmental Stewardship is Good Policy, and Good Politics

"Nothing is more conservative than conservation."- Russell Kirk

The 41st annual celebration of Earth Day took place in April, 2011. There is much to celebrate. Four decades ago, our country was a much dirtier place - today, the Cuyahoga River no longer burns.

Historically, the Republican Party has been a leader in the conservation movement. Today, we have a unique opportunity to champion policies that combine the strategic goal of energy independence with responsible environmental stewardship. A common sense energy policy based on increased efficiency and reduced consumption, coupled with environmental measures that will improve the quality of life in communities across our nation, is a strategy for victory in any election cycle.

A Legacy of Faithful Stewardship

Today, it often seems that the political left is the champions of the environment, the ones driving the policy agenda on a range of issues. But this hasn't always been so - indeed, Republicans are responsible for many of the greatest environmental policy achievements in our nation's history. This should not be surprising; there is no intrinsic hostility to environmental concerns in classical conservative political theory. One can, in other words, be both a good conservative, and a good environmentalist, at the same time.

Edmund Burke is one example of the harmony between a concern for the environment and traditional conservative thought. Burke, after all, placed a great emphasis on the existence of an "intergenerational contract" - a duty owed by the present to future generations. What can be more "conservative" then focusing on preserving society and extending it forward in time? And how can that be accomplished without a due concern for the health of the environment and the depletion, or exhaustion, of natural resources? As Pope Benedict XVI has observed, "[t]he environment is God's gift to everyone, and in our use of it we have a responsibility towards the poor, towards future generations, and towards humanity as a whole."[26]

In terms of past Republican environmental accomplishments, the presidency of Theodore Roosevelt immediately comes to mind. But there are many more. For example, it was a Republican president, Benjamin Harrison, who signed the law establishing our national forests in 1890. More recently, it was a Republican president, Richard Nixon, who created the Environmental Protection Agency (EPA) and signed the landmark Clean Air Act into law. His successor, Gerald Ford, gave our nation its first fuel efficiency standards, CAFE, which, to this day, saves millions of barrels of oil every year. Last, but certainly not least, President Reagan gets the credit for the Montreal Protocol -arguably one of the most critical international treaties ever signed - which phased out a number of chemical compounds damaging to the Earth's ozone layer.

Nor, has Republican leadership on environmental issues been limited to the executive branch. Rep. John Saylor (R-Pa), for example, co-sponsored the Wilderness Act of 1964 and, throughout his legislative career, was a champion of environmental and conservation legislation. Closer to my own home, Delaware's own Senator Bill Roth did extensive work on protecting Alaska's wilderness areas.

Opportunities Today

Today, however, the GOP's legacy of leadership on environmental issues is often forgotten. Instead, we have become the party opposed to the anthropogenic global warming "hoax." Environmentalism has become, for some conservatives, a dirty word, tinged with the negative connotations of a statist, anti-growth (or even, anti-human), radical agenda.

However, the Left's extreme, often dogmatic, positions on

31

many environmental issues create opportunities for the Republican party, if we rediscover our former role as advocates for faithful, common sense stewardship of the environment. As David Frum has observed, Republicans don't have to focus on the agendas of environmental advocacy groups in order to reach voters on environmental issues:

> "To [many voters], the environment means something different than it does to the Sierra Club. It's very much a quality of life (issue). When low income voters talk about the environment, they don't mean 'THE environment,' they mean 'MY environment.' The environment of the cities, six lane highways through new suburban developments, garbage dumps and toxins, things that have a very direct impact. It is precisely because the Republican Party does not buy into a lot of the apocalyptic fantasies of the environmental movement that it has the ability to reach these people in a common sense, non-fanatical way.

> The way you position the party is to say, Al Gore has been looking for ways to take away your car since 1972. Global warming is just the latest justification for doing something he wanted to do anyway. We are the party of a more common sense approach. We want to do what's necessary, but only what's necessary. For us, this is not a substitution for religion.

> I think it is often true that in politics, the party that ends up owning an issue is often the party that is less determined about the issue. For example, it was a Democratic president who ended up signing welfare reform because he could say to the voters that he was doing it as a pragmatic matter, not as an ideological

issue. In the same way, we can be the pragmatists on the environment and leave the job of being the ideologues to the Democrats."[27]

Newt Gingrich has observed the same opportunities and made them a keystone in his push for "Green Conservatism." Writing in Human Events in 2007, Gingrich noted that:

> "Over the last 36 years, I have watched the pro-regulation, pro-litigation, pro-taxation and pro-centralized-government advocates become the definers of environmentalism.
>
> The left would have us believe that to be an environmentalist you have to believe in catastrophic threats, dramatic increases in government power and economically draconian solutions. Such a big-government bureaucracy, trial-lawyer-litigation and excessive-regulation 'environmentalism' does a poor job of protecting the environment while it erodes individual freedom, destroys jobs and weakens our country.
>
> The time has come to propose a fundamentally different approach to a healthy environment and a healthy economy.
>
> The time has come for the development of a mainstream environmentalism as an alternative to big bureaucracy and big litigation environmentalism. You could call it 'green conservatism,' but it's really the mainstream environmental approach that has worked so well in the United States."

"Quality of Life" & Energy Independence

So what might this mainstream, common-sense, environmental agenda look like?

Locally, it encompasses a range of measures targeting quality of life issues - such as transportation, the rational planning of development, and the preservation of open space and the historic character of communities. In this regard, we must not be against development per se. Instead, we must strike an appropriate balance between the rights of property owners and the rights and interests of the broader community. Most importantly, we should plan ahead so that development does not have a negative impact on our local schools, our existing infrastructure, and our public services.

Nationally, it would also involve appropriately pricing energy so that it takes into account "externalities" that are ignored by the market. The Regional Greenhouse Gas Initiative (REGGI), a Republican idea that seeks to efficiently reduce greenhouse gas emissions, is a successful example of one such policy.[28]

Another key piece must be an honest discussion about energy independence. As Sen. Lindsey Graham has observed, "we are more dependent on foreign oil today than after 9/11. That is political malpractice, and every member of Congress is responsible."[29]

Simply put, our dependence on imported oil empowers regimes fundamentally hostile to our values, and our national interests. Regimes, for example, like "Saudi Arabia, the world's largest gas station and a medieval dictatorship that is a cash machine for terrorist bombers" whose "agenda is keeping us hooked on oil and avoiding uppity notions about energy diversification."[30]

The world's dependence on imported Gulf oil is also a major strategic vulnerability for the global economy. Saudi Arabia accounts for virtually all of the spare, or excess, oil production capacity in the world. That makes its oil facilities tempting targets for terrorists. The possibility of one, or more, catastrophic terrorist attacks on oil infrastructure targets in the Gulf remains one of our least-discussed strategic vulnerabilities. Thus, for a variety of reasons, "moving America towards a cleaner and more efficient energy economy is of the utmost importance to the nation's health, competitiveness, and security."[31]

Conclusion

In the words of David Jenkins, "rediscovering conservatism's green side is the path to reviving the popularity of conservative thought in America. This should not be hard to do. After all, this is a path that only requires embracing American conservatism's traditionalist roots and the stewardship ethic that lies at its core."[32]

Advancing a common-sense environmental agenda will pay political dividends for the GOP; it's also the right thing to do.

--

[26] Pope Benedict, XVI. (2009). Charity in Truth: Caritas in Veritate. (San Francisco: Ignatius Press), No. 48.

[27] Hawkins, John. (Jan. 30, 2008). "An Interview with David Frum." Right Wing News. Retrieved from: http://rightwingnews.com/mt331/2008/01/an_interview_with_david_frum_a.php

[28] Buntin, John. (Dec. 2010) "A Cap-and-Trade Program That Works." Governing.

[29] Friedman, Thomas L. (Feb. 27, 2010). "How the GOP Goes Green." The New York Times.

[30] DiPeso, Jim. (Dec. 13, 2009). "Case for Moving Away from Fossil Fuels Remains Clear." The Herald (Everett, WA).

[31] Yin, Clifton. (April 7, 2010). "Graham's Climate Change Courage." FrumForum. Retrieved from: http://www.frumforum.com/grahams-climate-change-courage

[32] Jenkins, David. (2009). "Conservatism's Green Roots." inFocus Quarterly. Vol. III, No. 3.

6.
Religion, Science & Climate Change: The Truth Can Never Be a Heresy

"And yet...it moves." - Galileo (attributed)

Do not be deceived. The opposition to the scientific evidence supporting anthropogenic global warming (AGW) among some conservatives may, at times, hide behind a pseudo-scientific veneer. However, much of it is often rooted in an anti-intellectual strain of religious fundamentalism. It is this element - a barren theology that leaves no room for our God-given gifts of reason and discovery - that gives the opposition its implacable character.

Some say faith and reason are at war in the modern age.

This is not so for men like Rep. John Shimkus, who premises his rejection of AGW on Scriptural passages promising that the Earth will not perish in a flood. For him, the war is over, and reason has been routed from the field.

Sadly, Rep. Shimkus is not alone. Many conservative opponents of AGW claim that it is impossible because God would never permit it, or that it is erroneous because only God, and not humanity, has the capacity to destroy the world. I suppose these individuals have never heard of nuclear weapons.

It is the religious aspect of the AGW debate that has taken it out of the realm of mere policy, and planted it firmly in the thick of the culture wars.

As a result, any understanding of the opposition to AGW or of the apparent anti-intellectualism in segments of the GOP today must begin with a discussion of religion and theology - specifically, the anti-intellectual theology underpinning elements of the fundamentalist Christian Right. In this regard, climate denial is merely one aspect of a broader rejection of reason and scientific inquiry.

With respect to the environment, these theological strains tend to place great emphasis on humanity's "dominion" over the Earth, but downplay or entirely ignore our concomitant responsibility for the stewardship of it. In so doing, they provide a false reading of the Book of Genesis, one that ignores the connotations of nurturing and care present in the original Hebrew text in favor of an interpretation emphasizing naked power and supremacy. Simply put, the Biblical mandate is to care for creation, not to commodify and exploit it.

In addition, AGW also touches on millennialist currents and visions prevalent in some streams of fundamentalist Christianity. This is significant. Stewardship is rooted in a concern for the future well-being of others. It matters little to those who believe our world has no future, or that God will miraculously deliver them from it, and its consequences. Like the Easter Islanders of old, many among us seem ready to bet that the *moai* will come to life and rescue us from ourselves. In the face of very real problems, such an escape into magical thinking may temporarily relieve anxiety, but it actually accelerates the trajectory towards disaster.

In its opposition to AGW, the anti-intellectual theological strain also ignores the first of the cardinal virtues - prudence. According to the United States Council of Catholic Bishops, "[p]rudence is intelligence applied to our actions... a thoughtful, deliberate, and reasoned basis for taking or avoiding action to achieve a moral good."[33] Prudence speaks to the need for sagacity, for careful reflection and consideration. It is a requisite for effective stewardship, and effective political leadership.

Today, there is no debate in the scientific community about whether the Earth is warming - it is. There is also a nearly unanimous consensus that human activity is responsible for this warming. There is some debate over the severity of the consequences that will inure from this and, on the margins, over whether we can take any remedial measures that will slow, stop, or reverse this process. The consensus position, however, is clear - it will probably have a significant negative impact on human civilization and the natural world, and there are practical steps that could be taken now to avoid this fate.

Given the potential implications for humanity, it is reckless to ignore the broad scientific consensus on AGW. Doing so in the face of this evidence is tantamount to an abdication of both our duty to future generations and our duty to care for the natural world. It is an act of immense selfishness. After all, the natural world - our Earth - is a shared, common inheritance. As the late Admiral Hyman Rickover once said: "A prudent and responsible parent will use his capital sparingly in order to pass on to his children as much as possible of his inheritance. A selfish and irresponsible parent will squander it in riotous living and care not one whit how his offspring will fare."

Placing religion and theology in the service of such selfishness and irresponsibility is an act of deep betrayal.

In the end, a theology that requires the rejection of empirical evidence on a variety of topics, and an escapist descent into magical thinking, is not a living faith. It is a dead one. Such a faith is not spiritual armor for the believer going out into the world, but rather, an intellectual tomb for someone hiding from it.

Let me suggest something different. Faith and reason are not at war —or at least, do not need to be. Religious belief and rational inquiry, faith and doubt, are not binary pairs of opposites. Indeed, at a fundamental level, both religion and science remind us of the deep mystery underpinning the world and our existence in it. Scientific inquiry also expands our knowledge of the natural world and the universe which, as we are told in Genesis, is a reflection of God. This is why learning, the quest for knowledge and understanding, is a sacred thing. As Pope Benedict XVI has taught, religious faith "consolidates, integrates and illuminates truth[s] acquired by human reason."[34] For my own part, I think God gave us our minds, our intellect, and our capacity to reason in the hope that we would put them to use advancing the common good.

Today, in their opposition to AGW, some religious conservatives imagine themselves as brave dissenters defending individual rights and Biblical truth from yet another assault by a grasping, rapacious, regulatory government and the atheist liberals that run it. They are wrong. They are actually reprising the role of the Inquisition in the trial of Galileo.

And in so doing, they have forgotten something fundamental about faith. If God is the author of the world, then the truth, whatever it is, can never be a heresy...and people of faith ought never fear it.

--

[33] "Prudence, Poverty, the Common Good, and Solidarity." Catholic Climate Covenant. Retrieved from: http://catholicclimatecovenant.org/catholic-teachings/

[34] Rome Reports. "Pope says faith and reason have a 'complimentary relationship.'" (June 16, 2010). Retrieved from: http://www.romereports.com/palio/Pope-says-faith-and-reason-have-a-complementary-relationship-english-2295.html

7.

The Republican Case for Passenger Rail

A record 28.7 million people traveled on Amtrak passenger trains in fiscal year 2010. Despite this, Congressional Republicans have targeted federal support of passenger rail transportation for elimination. Overall, the Spending Reduction Act of 2011 proposed by the Republican Study Committee would end $1.565 billion in annual federal operating subsidies for Amtrak as well as $2.5 billion in intercity and high-speed rail grants. The elimination of Amtrak's federal subsidy could result in the end of intercity passenger rail operations in the United States. In so doing, Congressional Republicans risk sacrificing our nation's long-term interests in favor of a rigid, doctrinaire adherence to ideology.

Amtrak (formally known as the National Passenger Rail Corporation) is a government-owned corporation formed in 1971 by the Nixon administration to take over increasingly unprofitable intercity passenger rail service that had previously been operated, at a significant loss, by private railroads. It has been heavily dependent on federal subsidies throughout its entire existence. Amtrak, and funding for passenger rail projects in general, has long been a target of conservatives. In particular, conservatives point to Amtrak's dependence on federal subsidies and its inability to be "self-sufficient" or "profitable." For many on the Right, "subsidy" is simply a dirty word.

According to former Amtrak President Alex Kummant, however, conservative criticism of passenger rail, "needs serious re-examination, because national transportation strategy is an issue of US national competitiveness, and passenger rail has a significant role to play... A major federal government role in building and maintaining significant national assets that make the country competitive is entirely consistent with conservative philosophy."[35] Writing in The Atlantic Monthly, Richard Florida has made a similar point:

> "It's time to start thinking of our transit and infrastructure projects less in political terms and more as a set of strategic investments that are fundamental to the speed and scope of our economic recovery and to the new, more expansive economic geography required for long-run growth and prosperity."[36]

Indeed, the conservative fixation on "self-sufficiency" ignores the role historically played by government, at all levels, in developing our nation's transportation infrastructure - from the canal, rail, and road building of the early/mid 19th Century, to the construction of the Interstate Highway system beginning in the 1950's, to the High Speed Rail Corridors project today. As one commentator has noted, "[s]ince the days of the ancient Greeks, government has subsidized transportation, building lighthouses and roads, dredging rivers, and so on."[37]

When it comes to passenger rail, conservatives are in desperate need of a paradigm shift; instead of framing the debate in terms of "self-sufficiency" and profitability, conservatives should focus on the economic value of strategic investments in our transportation infrastructure. Simply put, no passenger rail system in the entire developed world is "self-sufficient" - all require some form of public support. However, this is not a condemnation of passenger rail. Self-sufficiency is not the standard we utilize to gauge the value of other transportation modes in our economy. Both civil aviation and our nation's highways benefit from a range of public subsidies and support - both direct, and indirect. Indeed, a case can be made that civil aviation is one of the most heavily subsidized industries in our nation today.

In the end, passenger rail provides a public service. And profitability, or "self-sufficiency," is not the most useful metric when gauging the value of public services.

In addition, passenger rail provides a number of benefits to our economy. It plays a critical role, particularly in the Northeast Corridor region and in California, in reducing traffic congestion on our roadways, it reduces pollution and gasoline consumption, and it helps to reduce overall travel costs. These benefits would only increase if critical investments in modernizing our rail infrastructure, such as the High Speed Rail Corridors projects, were made.

In 2008, Congress passed the Passenger Rail Investment and Improvement Act (PRIIA) which, among other things, established a high-speed rail corridor development program. The viability of many of the designated high-speed rail corridors is amply documented by research - indeed, many of these projects have been on the drawing board, or under consideration, for years. PRIIA represented a forward-looking, strategic investment in our transportation infrastructure - one that will bring significant economic benefits to a diverse range of communities across the nation.

In his State of the Union speech on January 25, 2011, President Obama reaffirmed his commitment to high speed rail, saying "[w]ithin 25 years, our goal is to give 80 percent of Americans access to high-speed rail." The President's vision of developing a state-of-the-art, high speed rail passenger system is one Republicans should embrace. The High Speed Rail Corridors project is a long overdue recognition of a simple fact - a modern transportation system requires a modern infrastructure. In a way, it is to passenger rail what the development of the Interstate Highway system was the automobile.

It is time for conservatives to reconsider their historic opposition to federal funding for passenger rail. As Kummant has noted, "[t]he current approach of the right, basically ignoring the national competitiveness implications of transportation and the related energy issues, is an abdication of responsibility."[38] Stripping a critical link from our nation's transportation system at this juncture will impede economic growth and recovery, and damage our competitiveness. That is the last thing we ought to do. Indeed, today - a time of rising fuel costs and increasing global economic pressures - is actually the time to invest in developing a state-of-the-art 21st Century passenger rail infrastructure that will be the envy of the world.[39]

--

[35]Kummant, Alex. (Sep. 12, 2009). "Passenger Rail: A New Conservative Position." American Thinker.

[36] Florida, Richard. (May 4, 2009). "Mega-Regions and High-Speed Rail." The Atlantic Monthly. Retrieved from: http://www.theatlantic.com/national/archive/2009/05/mega-regions-and-high-speed-rail/17006/

[37] Loving, Jr., Rush. (Feb. 15, 2009). "Why Amtrak Can't- and Never Will- Make Money." Richmond Times-Dispatch.

[38]Kummant, "Passenger Rail."

[39]This essay was originally posted at FrumForum (http://www.frumforum.com/put-high-speed-rail-on-the-fast-track) and at TommyWonk (http://www.tommywonk.com/2011/02/republican-case-for-amtrak-and-high.html)

8.

Death in Judgment: Reflections on Capital Punishment

"Many that live deserve death. And some that die deserve life. Can you give it to them? Then do not be too eager to deal out death in judgment. For even the very wise cannot see all ends."- J.R.R. Tolkien

A report released by Amnesty International in March 2011, shows that the number of executions world-wide fell in 2010. Regrettably, however, the United States continues to be a global leader in capital punishment.[40]

The release of the Amnesty International report creates an opportunity for renewed focus and discussion about capital punishment in America. Simply put, the time has come for the United States to abandon capital punishment as a criminal penal sanction. The continued practice of capital punishment separates the United States from its democratic peers. Moreover, it is a policy that is increasingly indefensible in light of the risk of wrongful convictions and the evidence of discrimination and arbitrariness in capital sentencing.

The moral horizon

As a conservative who believes in an enduring moral order, it is appropriate for me to begin this discussion with a brief examination of the morality of capital punishment in general.

In this regard, the *Catechism of the Catholic Church* states:

> "Assuming that the guilty party's identity and responsibility have been fully determined, the traditional teaching of the Church does not exclude recourse to the death penalty, if this is the only possible way of effectively defending human lives against the unjust aggressor.
>
> If, however, non-lethal means are sufficient to defend and protect people's safety from the aggressor, authority will limit itself to such means, as these are more in keeping with the concrete conditions of the common good and more in conformity with the dignity of the human person.
>
> Today, in fact, as a consequence of the possibilities which the state has for effectively preventing crime, by rendering one who has committed an offense incapable of doing harm—without definitively taking away from him the possibility of redeeming himself—the cases in which the execution of the offender is an absolute necessity 'are very rare, if not practically non-existent.'"

The Catholic Church is not alone in its opposition to capital punishment - many other Christian denominations have spoken out officially against the practice including, for example, the Evangelical Lutheran Church ("We increasingly question whether the death penalty has been and can be administered justly…. Our challenge is to incapacitate offenders in a manner that limits violence, and holds open the possibility of conversion and restoration…. The ongoing controversy surrounding the death penalty shows the weaknesses of its justifications. We would be a better society by joining the many nations that have already abolished capital punishment."),[41] the United Methodist Church ("We believe the death penalty denies the power of Christ to redeem, restore and transform all human beings… For this reason, we oppose the death penalty (capital punishment) and urge its elimination from all criminal codes"),[42] and the Episcopal Church ("The Church will continue to decry the revenge of state-sanctioned homicides. We abhor the racism and economic injustices evident in our criminal justice system.").[43]

The company we keep

Globally, there is a strong correlation between capital punishment and totalitarianism. Indeed, the United States is one of the last Western democracies that still carries out executions.

For example, as of this writing, only 3 (out of 50) nations in Europe retain the death penalty. One, Russia, has a moratorium on further executions. One, Latvia, has abolished capital punishment except during war. Only one – Belarus - continues to practice capital punishment in 2011. And Belarus is a petty thugocracy, not a liberal democracy.

In contrast, the United States annually ranks among the world's leaders in executions. 2010 was no exception. Last year, America ranked fifth globally in executions, behind China, Iran, North Korea, and Yemen, and ahead of Libya and Syria. With the sole exception of Taiwan, none of our industrial democracy peers are on the list. Such, apparently, is the company we keep.

One innocent life?

The first predicate to capital punishment is a criminal justice system capable of determining a guilty person's identity and culpability with the requisite level of certainty.

But what is the requisite level of certainty?

From 1976 to today, more than 1,200 offenders have been put to death in the United States. During this same period, almost 140 convicts on death row have been exonerated of their crimes.[44]

These figures are troubling. The number of individuals on death row that have been exonerated is almost 12% of the total number of offenders executed. As George Will noted in 2000, capital punishment in America "is a catalog of appalling miscarriages of justice, some of them nearly lethal. Their cumulative weight compels the conclusion that many innocent people are in prison, and innocent people have been executed."[45]

Arbitrary application

At the same time, other data point to systemic flaws in the application of the death penalty within our criminal justice system. In brief, there is evidence that socio-economic status, race (particularly of the victim), and even geography play key roles in who lives and who dies.

For example, since 1976, about 90% of the criminal defendants sentenced to death could not afford to hire their own lawyers. Puzzlingly, despite the fact that African American's account for half of all homicide victims, more than 75% of those sentenced to death in the United States were convicted for killing a Caucasian. As the Death Penalty Information Center has observed, study after study has found evidence of discrimination based on the race of the victim, the race of the defendant, or sometimes even both, in capital sentencing.[46]

Moreover, the death penalty is not applied evenly across the United States, or even uniformly within states that permit capital sentencing. Indeed, Texas alone accounts for over 38% of the capital sentences carried out since 1976. In fact, just three states, Texas, Virginia, and Oklahoma, combined account for well over half the total executions during the same period.[47]

Looking at the United States as a whole, the states of the former Confederacy accounted for 89% of our executions in 2008 (33 out of 37), 81% in 2009 (42 out of 52), and 70% in 2010 (32 out of 46). From 1976 to 2010, the former Confederacy accounted for more than 70% of all executions. Add in the civil war "border states" and Oklahoma, and it's more like 90%.

Today, the criminal most likely to be executed in America is a poor minority, represented by a public defender, convicted of killing a Caucasian in the South. It is impossible to separate this fact from the implications inherent in its historic context. As a result, in the words of David Gushee, "the death penalty is a public policy that fails the most basic standards of justice."[48]

Dollars & Sense

An additional argument against capital punishment is that a death sentence is more expensive than life without the possibility of parole.

For example, a 2005 report in the Los Angeles Times found that California incurred an additional $114,000,000 per year beyond the costs of life imprisonment due to the death penalty. Similarly, a study from 2002 determined that the costs of having the death penalty in Indiana exceed the cost of life without parole by roughly 38%. This is true, apparently, even in Texas, where a 1992 report by The Dallas Morning Herald noted that the costs of executing a convicted criminal were 2.5 greater then life imprisonment.[49]

These figures are not inconsequential - it would seem that a sentence of life without the possibility of parole actually saves the taxpayers money.

But what of deterrence?

The best argument summoned by defenders of capital punishment is that it plays a deterrent role - in other words, that having the death penalty on the books reduces violent crime.

I doubt it. First, the application of the penalty – death - is far too temporally removed from the criminal act at issue for the sanction to have much deterrent value. Typically, years pass between the conviction, and the application of the death sentence while the criminal defendant exhausts various appeals. Also, as noted above, the roles played by socio-economic status, race, and geography in sentencing, mitigate against any broad deterrent effect.

Crime data from the FBI supports the hypothesis that capital punishment does not deter violent crime. For example, in 2008, the average murder rate in states that had death penalty statutes was 5.2, whereas, by comparison, it was 3.3 in states that did not (rate is per 100,00 ppl). Moreover, each of the top 20 states, in terms of murder rate, in 2008, had the death penalty. 9 of the 15 states with lowest murder rate did not.[50]

None of this data suggests a deterrent effect.

Conclusion

Cardinal McCarrick, Archbishop of Washington, has written that "…the death penalty diminishes all of us, increases disrespect for human life, and offers the tragic illusion that we can teach that killing is wrong by killing."[51]

In 2003, the Texas Baptist Christian Life Commission issued a report examining capital punishment's scriptural basis and its operation and application in Texas. Based on its review, the Commission concluded that "biblical teaching does not support capital punishment as it is practiced in contemporary society…. The practice of capital punishment in our nation and state is an affront to biblical justice, both in terms of its impact on the marginalized in society and in terms of simple fairness."[52]

The Commission's conclusion is undoubtedly correct.

There is evidence that the death penalty is applied in a discriminatory and arbitrary fashion within the United States today. There is an unacceptable risk that innocent persons will be executed. And even the very worst criminals among us never cease to be human beings.

America should join the evolving Western moral consensus on this issue and abolish capital punishment. The law can be a teacher - here, let the lesson be that all human life has value.

--

[40] BBC News. (Mar. 27, 2011). "Amnesty International: Global death penalty trend falls." Retrieved from: http://www.bbc.co.uk/news/world-12868522

[41] Evangelical Lutheran Church in America. (Sept. 1991). "A social statement on: The Death Penalty." Retrieved from: http://www.elca.org/What-We-Believe/Social-Issues/Social-Statements/Death-Penalty.aspx

[42] United Methodist Church. (2004). The Book of Discipline of The United Methodist Church – 2004. (Nashville: United Methodist Publishing House).

[43] Episcopal Church. (June, 2001). "Minutes of the Executive Council Standing Committee on National Concerns." Retrieved from: http://www.episcopalchurch.org/gc/ccab/EC_NatConcerns_2001_06_0811.pdf

[44] Retrieved from: http://www.deathpenaltyinfo.org/documents/FactSheet.pdf

[45] Will, George F. (April 6, 2000). "The Death Penalty and Horrifying Mistakes." The Washington Post.

[46] Retrieved from: http://www.deathpenaltyinfo.org/documents/FactSheet.pdf

[47] Id.

[48] Gushe, David. (Feb. 8, 2007). "Time for a national death penalty moratorium." Associated Baptist Press.

[49] Hoppe, C. (Mar. 8, 1992). "Executions Cost Texas Millions." The Dallas Morning News, 1A.

[50] Retrieved from: http://www.deathpenaltyinfo.org/facts-about-deterrence-and-death-penalty

[51] Retrieved from: http://www.usccb.org/comm/archives/2002/02-062.shtml

[52] Texas Baptist Christian Life Commission. (Jan. 10, 2003). "Christians and Capital Punishment." Baptist General Convention of Texas. Retrieved from: http://www.bgct.org/TexasBaptists/Document.Doc?&id=1502

9.

Greater Opportunities for Love

Special education students are, all too often, the subject of jokes or humor. They, and their parents, are frequently misunderstood. Individuals with more severe disabilities are too often seen, at some level, as burdens both on their parents and on society in general. For all these reasons, special education, and the way we address the needs of all individuals with disabilities, raises important policy questions that go to the very heart of who we are as a people, of how we recognize the inherent dignity and worth of all human beings.

This issue is a very personal one for me, as I am a former public school special education student. In the early 1980's, special education lacked the emphasis on mainstreaming and integration that is present today. Instead, it was common for children with disabilities to be segregated away from the general education population, or clustered at specific locations. As a result, I did not attend my feeder-pattern elementary school until the middle of third grade. Instead, I rode the proverbial "short bus" to a centralized location where I was, for significant portions of the school day, in classes with only my disabled peers.

I was learning disabled but also gifted, so I was eventually able to exit special education and be totally mainstreamed back at my regular home school. Even so, I was not reading/writing at grade level until about 6th or 7th grade in middle school.

I wanted to share my own experiences particularly for the parents of special needs children. In my own life, it was a combination of loving parents and some excellent teachers who got me through some very difficult times and helped me along a path that took me from special education all the way to Duke Law School.

Obviously, my own story does not directly relate to children with more severe cognitive or physical impairments. However, loving parents and caring teachers have opportunities to help such children become as independent and as capable as they can be.

But it is a mistake to focus this discussion merely on what we can do for children with disabilities: they have much to offer all of us.

Many months ago, I read an article that discussed, in part, Sarah Palin's failure to connect with suburban voters in New York. I understand Palin is a divisive figure at this point, but let's put that aside for a moment and focus on one thing: her decision not to abort Trig after learning that he had Down syndrome. Part of the author's argument was that Palin's decision to have Trig was simply incomprehensible to many voters in communities where children with severe disabilities, such as Down syndrome, are simply aborted as a matter of course. Indeed, nationally, about 90% of the cases of Down syndrome diagnosed by prenatal testing are eliminated by abortion each year.[53]

Assuming this is true, what does it say about us as a civilization? What does it say about our future? At some point, will we create incentives and inducements to parents to simply abort children with severe disabilities in order to save society the "costs" of caring for them? Will we really, as the eugenicists of the early 20th century dreamed, "cull the herd" so to speak? And who, precisely, will we empower to decide which lives are worth living?

As Michael Gerson has written in the Washington Post:

> "The wrenching diagnosis of 47 chromosomes must seem to parents like the end of a dream instead of the beginning of a life. But children born with Down syndrome — who learn slowly but love deeply — are generally not experienced by their parents as a curse but as a complex blessing. And when allowed to survive, men and women with an extra chromosome experience themselves as people with abilities, limits and rights. Yet when Down syndrome is detected through testing, many parents report that genetic counselors and physicians emphasize the difficulties of raising a child with a disability and urge abortion.
>
> This is properly called eugenic abortion — the ending of 'imperfect' lives to remove the social, economic and emotional costs of their existence. And this practice cannot be separated from the broader social

63

treatment of people who have disabilities. By eliminating less perfect humans, deformity and disability become more pronounced and less acceptable. Those who escape the net of screening are often viewed as mistakes or burdens. A tragic choice becomes a presumption — 'Didn't you get an amnio?' — and then a prejudice. And this feeds a social Darwinism in which the stronger are regarded as better, the dependent are viewed as less valuable, and the weak must occasionally be culled."[54]

All this is based on a fundamental misconception- a propensity to see the disabled as "burdens" rather than as what they truly are: opportunities.

Yes - opportunities. As one of my heroes, the late Representative Henry Hyde put it, "a handicapped child is an even greater opportunity for love."

In an era that, falsely, celebrates the "Cult of Self" and that exults the autonomy and primacy of the individual above all else, we are too apt to forget the truth: that we are only really free when we set aside ourselves and live lives dedicated to the service of others. The disabled, the elderly, the poor, the most vulnerable among us - these populations remind us of this truth. They invite us to seize the opportunity to grow as human beings.

And in the end, such service is not an act of mere sympathy. It is not condescending. It is an act of love. And it is only in love and solidarity with one another that we all find freedom, dignity, and purpose.

The image attached to Michael Gerson's Washington Post article is of Charles de Gaulle - the Free French leader and post-war French President who was, in many ways, the perfect embodiment of Gallic arrogance. Few know that de Gaulle had a daughter – Annie - with Down syndrome. In Gerson's words, the image de Gaulle "rocking Anne in his arms at night speaks across the years." Would that we all heard its message - one of acceptance and love.

Our treatment of those with disabilities speaks to the very core of who we are as a people. There is no such thing as a life not worth living; no such thing as an "imperfect" human being. A civilization that thinks in such ways is not reaping the savings of burdens eliminated; it is impoverishing itself.

--

[53] Harmon, Amy. (May 9, 2007). "Prenatal Test Puts Down Syndrome in Hard Focus." The New York Times.

[54] Gerson, Michael. (Sept. 10, 2008). "Trig's Breakthrough." The Washington Post

10.

It's Time for Comprehensive Immigration Reform

In January, 2010, the United States Council of Catholic Bishops ("USCCB") launched a campaign in support of comprehensive immigration reform urging "Congress to take up as its next priority comprehensive immigration reform that would reunite families, regularize the status of an estimated 12 million people in this country illegally and restore due process protections for immigrants." The effort, although ultimately unsuccessful, was joined by leaders of other communities of faith.

The USCCB's call to action on this issue ought to be renewed. Simply put, comprehensive immigration reform that includes a path to legality ("earned legalization") for some of our nation's millions of illegal immigrants is long overdue. It is also my hope that the effort to reform our nation's immigration laws will enjoy bipartisan support that transcends the bitter divisions so prevalent in politics today.

America's immigration laws should serve our national interest while, at the same time, respecting the inherent human dignity of immigrants. These two principles complement one another. Our current, antiquated system does neither well. A pathway to legal status for some of our unauthorized immigrants must be a piece of any comprehensive immigration reform. At the same time, our federal government has a duty to secure our borders and enforce our immigration laws. An "earned legalization" program would not subvert these critical goals; on the contrary, it would further them.

It is critical to distinguish "earned legalization" from an "amnesty." Although specific proposals vary in some details, they typically require the payment of a fine, background checks, and the attainment some level of English language proficiency. Thus, "earned legalization" is not an amnesty; there is nothing automatic about it. Individuals participating in an earned legalization program will have to wait in line like any other immigrant. Meanwhile, they'll be asked to continue contributing to our society by paying taxes, starting businesses and being productive members within their communities.

As Senator John McCain noted in remarks concerning efforts to reform our immigration system in 2007, comprehensive reform that includes an "earned legalization" program is not a reward to law-breakers, but rather: "recognizes the problems inherent in the current system and provides a logical and effective means to address these problems... We have a national interest in identifying [unauthorized immigrants], incentivizing them to come forward out of the shadows, go through security background checks, pay back taxes, pay penalties for breaking the law, learn to speak English, and regularize their status. Anyone who thinks this goal can be achieved without providing an eventual path to a permanent legal status is not serious about solving this problem."[55]

Comprehensive immigration reform that includes both an "earned legalization" program and improved enforcement of our immigration laws would likely enjoy broad support. According to polling done over the past several years, a majority of Americans support the development of an earned legalization program done in conjunction with enhanced border security and internal enforcement. Polls show that a majority of Republican, Democratic and Independent voters support reform. At the same time, when given a choice, a majority favor "earned legalization" programs over an "enforcement-only" approach. This support for comprehensive reform has stayed consistent over time. As such, comprehensive reform that includes an "earned legalization" program would command legitimacy.

The absence of realistic alternatives also weighs heavily in favor of comprehensive reform and earned legalization. A massive round-up and deportation of the millions of unauthorized immigrants in the United States is not feasible from a practical perspective- as Sen. John McCain observed in 2006, "it would take 200,000 buses extending along a 1700 mile long line to deport 11 million people"- and would, if carried out, lead to immense human suffering and disruption to our own economy. It would also entail the disruption of well-established family units, the deportation of heads of households, and the removal of many United States citizen children born to undocumented parents.

Setting aside the human toll, such a policy would also be

extremely costly for the United States. According to U.S. Immigration Customs and Enforcement, rounding up and removing our undocumented population would cost as much as $100 billion dollars or more. Other estimates are higher, ranging up to $230 billion.[56] Long term, according to the Center for American Progress, the removal of our undocumented immigrant population would result in a cumulative $2.6 trillion drop in our GDP over a decade.

It is extremely unlikely that the people of the United States will ever countenance the type of "draconian police measures necessary" to identify, detain and deport such a large population,[57] nor that the federal government would ever be able to devote the resources necessary to accomplish such a task.

Given the foregoing, as Sen. Lindsey Graham noted in 2010, locating, deporting, or jailing, upwards of 12 million undocumented immigrants is neither a workable, nor a practical, solution.[58]

Comprehensive immigration reform could also be structured in a way that does justice to those who have complied with our laws and entered our nation legally and, thereafter, taken the actions necessary to remain in status. For example, in addition to being placed in the back of the line for legal permanent residency, participants in an "earned legalization" program could also be permanently barred from naturalizing and becoming U.S. citizens. Such a penalty affirms the seriousness of our immigration laws, does justice to those who have immigrated legally, and provides a disincentive to future illegal immigration.

Regardless, allowing the present status quo to continue indefinitely into the future is not a morally defensible course of action. As the USCCB has observed, an "immigration policy that allows people to live here and contribute to society for years but refuses to offer them the opportunity to achieve legal status does not serve the common good."[59]

Immigration policy is an issue of national significance. As such, the push for comprehensive reform should be a bipartisan effort. Republicans can look to the legacy of both President's Ronald Reagan and George W. Bush on this issue. Indeed, it is often forgotten that President Reagan supported the Immigration Reform and Control Act of 1986, legislation that included an amnesty for over 2 million unauthorized immigrants. At the same time, Democrats have the example set by the late Sen. Ted Kennedy on this issue, as well as, more recently, President Obama's (as yet still unfulfilled) campaign pledge to support reform.

Immigration policy has historically been a divisive issue nationally. All too often, "the immigration debate's harsh rhetoric makes scapegoats of immigrants" and dehumanizes them in various ways.[60] We each have an obligation, whatever our views on the merits of the issue may be, to help shape the tenor of the debate in a way that respects the fundamental human dignity of unauthorized immigrants.

For all these reasons, "comprehensive immigration reform is the only humane solution to the problem of illegal immigration."[61] Today, working together, an opportunity exists to address, and resolve, a long-standing problem for our nation. We must seize it, and enact bipartisan comprehensive immigration reform.

--

[55] This quote appears in a May 13, 2005 press release issued by Sen. McCain titled "Members of Congress Introduce Comprehensive Border Security & Immigration Reform Bill [S 2611]."

[56] According to a study done by the Center for American Progress, locating, securing, and deporting 10 million undocumented immigrants in a five-year period would cost between $206 & $230 billion dollars- or about $41.6 billion annually. By way of comparison, the budget for the entire federal Department of Homeland Security in 2008 was merely $47 billion.

[57] Will, George F. (Mar. 30, 2006). "Guard the Borders- And Face Facts Too." The Washington Post.

[58] Mahendra, Jackie. (Jan. 30, 2010). "Senator Graham: Deporting 12 Million Won't Work, Need a Comprehensive Immigration Fix." America's Voice. Retrieved from: http://americasvoiceonline.org/blog/entry/senator_graham_deporting_12_million_wont_work_need_a_comprehensive_imm/

[59] Retrieved from: http://www.justiceforimmigrants.org/documents/understanding-cst.pdf

[60] Appleby, J. Kevin. (Mar. 19, 2007). "Toward Immigration Reform." America Magazine, Vol. 196 No. 10.

[61] Id.

11.

Casting Out Fear in the Immigration Debate

There is no fear in love, but perfect love drives out fear because fear has to do with punishment, and so one who fears is not yet perfect in love. We love because He first loved us. If anyone says, "I love God," but hates his brother, he is a liar; for whoever does not love a brother whom he has seen cannot love God whom he has not seen. This is the commandment we have from him: whoever loves God must also love his brother.
- 1 John 4:18-21

At present, our nation has somewhere between 10 and 12 million (or more) unauthorized immigrants - roughly the equivalent of the population of Ohio, Pennsylvania, or Illinois. The majority of these individuals have been in the United States for 5 years or more. Many have children who are United States citizens, and many have other deep ties to their communities. Some say they are drawn here by jobs, and this is certainly true - economic opportunity, after all, and the chance to build a better life free from repression was the magnet that drew so many of our own ancestors to the New World.

The question of what to do with this enormous population is one of the most complicated, and emotionally charged, public policy questions facing us today. In particular, immigration policy is inextricably linked with demographic change and the diversification of America. It demands a sensitive and sophisticated approach. However, all to often, the debate is marked by extremism on both sides - by calls for essentially open borders and no consequences from the far left, to calls for mass deportation and removal by the far right, who focus solely on enforcement.

Religious leaders are in the vanguard

Today, religious leaders from a wide range of faiths, particularly Roman Catholics and Protestant Evangelicals, are in the vanguard of the push for reform.

For example, in May, 2010, the National Association of Evangelicals ran an advertisement in *Roll Call* calling for bipartisan immigration reform that "[r]espects the God-given dignity of every person; [p]rotects the unity of the immediate family; [r]espects the rule of law; [g]uarantees secure national borders; [e]nsures fairness to taxpayers; [and] establishes a path toward legal status and/or citizenship for those who qualify and who wish to become permanent residents."[62]

Earlier in 2010, Galen Carey, the Director of Government Affairs for the NEA, elaborated the basis of the NEA's support for immigration reform in an op-ed piece that appeared in The Washington Post.[63] In Carey's view:

"Our current system contradicts our nation's deepest values. The teachings of almost every religious tradition uphold the virtue of corporate as well as individual hospitality...

In the end, our nation's greatness will be marked by how we treat the most vulnerable, including the stranger, among us."

Meanwhile, Catholic leaders have also been active in pushing for reform. In the words of the Most Reverend Dennis M. Schnurr, Archbishop of Cincinnati: "We bishops are trying to be clear in expressing the basic moral principles involved in efforts to reform our immigration laws. These moral principles are founded on the inherent, God-given dignity of the human person."

Our religious leaders also recognize the implications of demonizing and dehumanizing immigrants. Richard Land, the head of the Southern Baptist Convention's Ethics & Religious Liberty Commission, has articulated the nexus between reform and our future as a society with particular clarity. Land perceives the danger posed to all of us by the poisoned debate over immigration reform. He has warned that the failure to pass comprehensive reform might "rend the fabric of our society." In his eyes, "[t]his is a moral issue. It's an issue that ... must be dealt with or it's going to lead to deep fissures in our society."[64]

Slouching towards Bexhill

One does not need to be clairvoyant to perceive the looming peril of Land's "deep fissures" and their potential consequences.

According to the author of Arizona's SB 1070, State Sen. Russell Pearce, and his circle of supporters, the "next battle" over immigration involves the so-called "anchor babies"- a dehumanizing, racist, and repugnant term used by far too many to describe the children of unauthorized immigrants that are born in the United States. Under the 14th Amendment, anyone born in the United States automatically becomes a United States citizen. This annoys and angers men like Sen. Pearce. In Pearce's view, such children should be denied citizenship, the 14th Amendment be damned. As the Arizona Business Journal reports, Pearce and his "state and national cohorts want to go after 'anchor babies' who are born here. They want to deny them services and reduce the costs associated with them. The immigration hardliners also want some kind of Arizona law on the books to spark a court fight and use our state as a test case to weaken the 14th Amendment."[65]

By "services" they mean such things as emergency medical care and free access to public education.

Again, these moves "signal the next steps for Pearce and immigration hawks across the nation: redefining citizenship and targeting the children of illegal immigrants."[66]

Such harshness isn't surprising; Pearce is on the record as believing that unauthorized immigrants *have no civil rights whatsoever.* In 2006, he stated, in response to a protest march, that "[t]hey're illegal and they have no right to be marching down our streets. *They have no constitutional rights. They don't have First-, Fourth-, Sixth amendment rights.* They're here illegally and they chose to be here illegally." (emphasis added).[67]

Pearce's vision would lead not to the disappearance of unauthorized immigrants but rather to the creation of a permanent, brutalized, Helot underclass. And of course, it would be a predominantly Hispanic one.

But our future Helot servants are not the only ones in peril, for only souls already brutalized would think of, or support, such extreme policies in the first place.

Reflecting on Pearce also makes something else clear: it is impossible to separate the debate over immigration reform from white fears about demographic and cultural change. The two are inextricably linked. I know that this is upsetting to some; and I know such fears do not animate each and every opponent of reform; but they are the background against which this debate is unfolding.

Again, one only has to look at the author of Arizona's SB 1070, the man promoting even harsher legislation and an attack on the 14th Amendment today, State Sen. Russell Pearce, to see the racial implications. As has been widely reported, Sen. Pearce openly associates with neo-Nazi/white nationalist leaders in Arizona, including a man named J.T. Ready.[68] In the words of one report from 2007, "Ready's tight with state Representative Russell Pearce, who's bashed Mexicans ever since a Latino teen shot off his finger when he was a county sheriff's deputy. Pearce is a racist law machine, pumping out statute after statute targeting the brown segment of AZ's population. At a June anti-illegal demonstration at the state Capitol, Ready and Pearce worked the crowd arm-in-arm."[69]

Pearce's relationship with Ready is a long and sordid tale.

Pearce was present at Ready's baptism into the Church of Jesus Christ of Latter-day Saints.[70] Subsequently, in 2006, Pearce endorsed Ready when the latter ran for a seat on the Mesa (Arizona) City Council. That same year, Pearce was apparently warned about Ready's connections to white supremacist groups by Bill Strauss, the local regional director for the Anti-Defamation League. Any ambiguity about Ready was removed in March, 2007, when Ready's racist activities were brought up in a legislative hearing and widely reported in the local media. Thus, the June 2007 anti-immigrant rally in Phoenix at which Pearce and Ready "worked the crowd" together is particularly significant, because it occurred after Ready was exposed as a white supremacist leader. [71]

Nor is Pearce's association with Ready an anomaly. In 2006, Sen. Pearce forwarded a racist e-mail from a neo-Nazi group to many of his friends and supporters.[72] Specifically, Pearce "sent out an e-mail that contained an article produced by the National Alliance, a neo-Nazi group known for its anti-Semitic views." The article dealt with "Jewish control of the news media and the media's bias against whites, while favoring minorities and Israel."[73]

The National Alliance, by the way, is the same group that brought us *The Turner Diaries* - an extremist work about an anti-Semitic race war that leads to the expulsion of all non-whites from America - the very book that helped push Timothy McVeigh towards the Oklahoma City bombing. A copy of a passage from the book was found in the car McVeigh drove on the day of the bombing. And "we're starting the Turner diaries early" were the words spoken by John William King as he chained James Byrd to his truck on a dark night in Jasper, Texas before dragging him to his death.[74]

The passage of SB 1070 created a climate in which other would-be leaders felt free to give vent to their xenophobic fantasies. For example, Tom Mullins, a 2010 Republican candidate for Congress from New Mexico, suggested in a radio interview that the Mexican border be mined.[75] Rep. Duncan Hunter of California opined that the U.S. born children of unauthorized immigrants - children that are US citizens - be deported.[76]

Future studies is a very imprecise field but as I look into my own crystal ball and consider all this, I wonder about the consequences of adopting a "fortress" mentality here in America, particularly given the racial overtones. What if the Tom Mullins' of the world prevail - will we be secure behind their minefields from whatever perils, real or imagined, lurk to the south?

I doubt it. Mullins' "Fortress America" mentality offers no promise for a brighter future. He'd make America the ultimate "gated community" separated from the anarchic violence and poverty characteristic of lands to our south by his minefield and his wall.

But order and stability cannot survive long under siege in isolated pockets. Nor is a fortress mentality healthy for us, because hidden away behind our gates, our minefields, and our walls, we will quickly loose our own humanity. Indeed, we lose much of what is best in our cultural heritage the moment we modify the 14th Amendment and affix the appellation *"homo sacer"*[77] to the 10-12 million people living and working here unlawfully. This is why, for me, it all goes back to human dignity and love - not a naive love but, rather, one born of the conviction that we are all brothers, after all, and that we bear a responsibility for each other.

There is no fear in love

In the words of the Apostle John, "there is no fear in love."[78] In the end, no matter our race, no matter our national origin, no matter our religion, we are all brothers and sisters under the same God. We are all equal in any way that matters. This does not mean we should have open borders, or neglect the enforcement of our immigration laws; nor does it mean that past violations of the law should be forgiven without consequences. It does mean we should take reasonable steps to bring millions out of the shadows. It does mean that we should respect the basic human dignity of our unauthorized immigrant population.

Make no mistake about it, the nativists and xenophobes will lead us to a very dark place, if we follow them. But a path to a more decent common future beckons. My prayer is that we cast out fear and, together, have the courage to secure that better future for our country.

--

[62] Strode, Tom. (May 13, 2010). "Fed. Action on immigration urged by Land, coalition." The Ethics and Religious Liberty Commission of the Southern Baptist Convention. Retrieved from: http://erlc.com/article/fed.-action-on-immigration-urged-by-land-coalition/

[63] Carey, Galen. (Jan. 28, 2010). "Why evangelicals want immigration reform this year." The Washington Post.

[64] Khimm, Suzy. (June 1, 2010) "A Right-Wing Schism Over Immigration Reform?" Mother Jones. Retrieved from: http://motherjones.com/politics/2010/05/right-wing-clash-over-immigration-reform

[65] Sunnucks, Mike. (June 21, 2010). "Next immigration fight takes

on 14th Amendment." Phoenix Business Journal. Retrieved from: http://www.bizjournals.com/phoenix/blog/business/2010/06/next_ immigration_ fight_takes_on_14th_amendment.html

[66] del Puerto, Luige. (June 4, 2010). "Born Illegal." Arizona Capital Times. Indeed, in early 2011, Sen. Pearce proposed new legislation in Arizona, SB 1611, that, although ultimately unsuccessful, sought to bar illegal immigrant children from attending public secondary schools and universities there. See Fisher, Howard. (Feb. 28, 2011). "Pearce moves to officially ban illegal immigrants from schools, driving." East Valley Tribune.

[67]Neiwert, David. (April 15, 2006). "Immigration and eliminationism." Retrieved from: http://dneiwert.blogspot.com/2006/04/ immigration-and-eliminationism.html

[68] Lemons, Stephen. (Nov. 22, 2007). "Racist Daisy-Chain." Phoenix New Times. Retrieved from: http://www.phoenixnewtimes. com/2007-11-22/news/racist-daisy-chain/

[69] Id.

[70] Lemons, Stephen. (Dec. 16, 2010). "When Valley Neo-Nazi J.T. Ready converted to Mormonism, Guess Which Prominent Politico Ordained Him an 'Elder.'" Phoenix New Times. Retrieved from: http://www.phoenixnewtimes.com/2010-12-16/news/webline/

[71] H., Robert. (Jan. 3, 2011). "Exclusive Footage: Sen. Russell Pearce endorsed JT Ready." Desert Free Press. Retrieved from: http://www. desertfreepress.com/content/exclusive-footage-sen-russell-pearce-endorsed-jt-ready. See also: Neiwart, David. (April 27, 2010). "Profiling Arizona legislator Russell Pearce: Author of immigration law is pals with noted neo-Nazi." Crooks and Liars. Retrieved from: http:// crooksandliars.com/david-neiwert/profiling-arizona-legislator-russell

[72] Sunnucks, Mike. (Oct. 10, 2006). "State lawmaker under fire for citing neo-Nazi article in e-mail." Phoenix Business Journal. Retrieved from: http://www.bizjournals.com/phoenix/stories/2006/10/09/daily22.html?surround=lfn

[73] Id.

[74] Anti-Defamation League. (June 10, 2008). "Aryan Brotherhood & the Turner Diaries." Retrieved from: http://www.adl.org/presrele/hatcr_51/3177-51.asp

[75] Huffington Post. (June 15, 2010). "Tom Mullins: New Mexico Congressional Candidate Wants Landmines Along U.S.-Mexico Border." Retrieved from: http://www.huffingtonpost.com/2010/06/15/tom-mullins-new-mexico-co_n_612482.html

[76] Los Angeles Times. (April 28, 2010). "Rep. Duncan Hunter backs deporting U.S.-born children of undocumented immigrants."

[77] The Italian philosopher Giorgio Agemben has used the old Roman term "homo sacer" to denote a state of permanent exception and exclusion applied by the law to certain groups of people. A graphic representation of the concept, applied in the immigration context, can be seen in the movie Children of Men.

[78] 1 John 4:18

12.

California Dreamin':
The Ghost of
Proposition 187
Continues to Haunt
the GOP

In 1994, California residents approved Proposition 187. The measure, supported by many California Republicans including then-Governor Pete Wilson, barred undocumented immigrants from utilizing various social services, including public education.

Ultimately, a federal district court determined that Proposition 187 was determined unconstitutional.

The Republican Party's embrace of Proposition 187 was extremely short-sighted. As the GOP was taking a nativist, xenophobic turn, California's electorate was becoming increasingly diverse. According to one author, "Governor Wilson's crusade against all immigrants, though later refined specifically to illegal aliens, alienated the bulk of California's fastest growing population, the Mexican origin slice of the state... The enthusiastic support of Proposition 187, a highly dubious effort fueled by rabid anti-Mexicans, of the state Republican Party drove away hundreds of thousands of Mexican Americans, including many who had climbed into the state's middle-class. Professor Bruce Cain of UC Berkeley reports that Mexican American men were re-registering Republican at a 50% rate before Proposition 187. That ended with Proposition 187."[79]

Although Governor Wilson was able to ride California's wave of anti-immigrant hysteria to victory in 1994, since that time no Republican presidential candidate has carried California. Indeed, since 1994, only one Republican has won a statewide race in California, and he had a neural net processor and a hyper-alloy combat chassis, at least in some of his most movies.[80] Overall, the California Republican Party has struggled to remain competitive. Today, Republicans do not have a registration majority in any of California's congressional districts. Even worse, Republican primaries in California, which still often feature an emphasis on illegal immigration and rhetoric echoing themes raised in the campaign for Proposition 187, "have a nasty habit of rendering their winners unelectable in November."[81] As a result, in retrospect, Governor Wilson's 1994 victory, and the passage of Proposition 187, may be "the most pyrrhic [victory] in modern American politics."[82]

Sadly, these are largely self-inflicted wounds.

Amnesia is a mental condition in which memory is disturbed or lost. The far right's love affair with Arizona's SB 1070 in 2010 was an example of political amnesia of the most severe kind. The rush to embrace SB 1070 ignored the lessons of Proposition 187.

Like California in 1994, Arizona's electorate is becoming more diverse. The number of Hispanic voters will continue to grow. This is why, long-term, support for measures like SB 1070 is a losing strategy, both locally in Arizona and nationally.

As Judge Napolitano noted on Fox News, by signing SB 1070, Governor Jan Brewer set a course that could bankrupt her state financially and the GOP politically:

> "Hispanics — who have a natural home in the Republican Party because they are socially conservative — will flee in droves. She's also gonna bankrupt her state, because no insurance company will provide coverage for this. And for all the lawsuits that will happen — for all the people that are wrongfully stopped — her budget will be paying for it. Her budget will be paying the legal bills of the lawyers who sue on behalf of those that were stopped."[83]

Although the enforcement of key portions of Arizona's draconian immigration statute has been stayed by a federal judge (a ruling that has been, as of this writing, upheld by the Federal Court of Appeals for Ninth Circuit),[84] politically, the damage has already been done.

Today, the tired, nativist rhetoric against undocumented immigrants may still get applause, but it is a long-term prescription for political irrelevancy. That is because, due to rapidly changing demographics in the United States, it is essential for the GOP to attracted larger numbers of Asian and Hispanic voters if it hopes to remain competitive in national elections, as well as within key states. The obvious racial overtones inherent in dehumanizing and demonizing a population of largely Hispanic and Asian undocumented immigrants renders this all but impossible to do.

Nationally, as the Wall Street Journal has noted, "[i]f current demographic and voting trends continue, Hispanics' growing share of the electorate could make Republican electoral college victories a near impossibility as early as 2020."85 Or as Whit Ayres put it in the Washington Post, "[i]f Republicans don't do better among Hispanics, we're not going to be talking about how to get Florida back in the Republican column, we're going to be talking about how not to lose Texas."86 As a result, "[a] party that thinks it can win elections by alienating Latinos is going to be in the minority for a very long time."87

Immigration panics come and go but, as the California example shows, the long-term costs of embracing them can be high. All of my fellow Republicans that rushed to embrace Arizona's SB 1070 would do well to remember the fate of the California GOP following the passage of Proposition 187.

After all, it would be a shame if, in the end, our collective political epithet was "*died of a panic.*"

--

[79] Contreras, Raoul Lowery. (Aug. 16, 2002). "The death of the California GOP." Calnews.com.

[80] "The Terminator." (1984).

[81] Meyerson, Harold. (June 10, 2010). "Calif. GOP primary winners look headed for defeat." The Washington Post.

[82] Id.

[83] The Raw Story. (April 24, 2010). "Judge Napolitano: Immigration law will 'bankrupt the Republican Party.'" Retrieved from: http://www.rawstory.com/rs/2010/04/24/judge-napolitano-immigration-law-bankrupt-republican-party/

[84] Fernandez, Valeria. (April 13, 2011). "Despite Latest Ruling, Immigrants Still Besieged in Arizona." New American Media.

[85] Wallsten, Peter. (Feb. 22, 2010). "GOP's Demographic Wager: Courting Latino Candidates." The Wall Street Journal, sec. A4.

[86] Slevin, Peter. (Feb. 21, 2010). "Republicans look to rebuild their traction with Hispanic voters." The Washington Post.

[87] The Wall Street Journal. (Aug. 30, 2008). "Immigrants and the GOP." A10.

13.

"Manning Up"? Speaking the Truth with Courage and Conviction

In November 2010, Joe Scarborough, a conservative television host on MSNBC, called on national Republicans to "man up" and confront Sarah Palin.[88]

I want to propose something rather different. The rise of politicians like Sarah Palin is merely a symptom of the radicalization of the political Right in America. As such, the real need is for people of good will to "man up" and speak honestly about the mass movement that supports and sustains politicians such as Palin - the Tea Party - and the broader cultural forces that have given rise to it and that continue to fuel it today.

Love demands candor; sometimes, certain truths must be plainly spoken. Although I agree with some positions held by the Tea Party movement and share many of its concerns regarding the direction of the country, I am convinced that its emergence represents a real danger to our common future. Indeed, I am persuaded that its course runs inevitably to a dystopian tomorrow.

Why? Because it is marked by anti-intellectualism, hostility to established institutions, resentment, and, most significantly, fear and anger. This fear is inchoate, but ever-present. At its base, I think it is a fear of the future - of the economic, demographic and cultural changes sweeping both our nation and the globe. In other words, it is a fear of the unknown.

And being fearful, it is brittle. As a result, it is intolerant of dissent and the open discussion and debate of ideas. This intolerance is expressed in naked hostility towards opponents - they are not merely wrong, they must be demonized. Above all else, it is marked by the utter absence of love, by which I mean that love of brother - *agape* - that is, for me, always truth's handmaiden.

Animated by fear and resentment, it is not surprising that another defining characteristic of the Tea Party is anger. Of course, many of its defenders will argue that this anger is the natural outgrowth of legitimate frustrations, of the perception held by many that they do not have a voice in affairs, or an understandable reaction to the mismanagement of the country. I disagree. Anger is a very dangerous thing - it corrodes, it pollutes, it distorts and it twists. It is ultimately more destructive to its bearer then to its object. In a political sense, there is a difference between anger and a thirst for righteousness, or a hunger for justice.

It would be a mistake, though, to believe that the political manifestations of fear and anger are uniquely the province of the Right. The Left has been marked by this as well - it evidenced a similar rush to demonize and vilify opponents, the same withholding of trust and respect, the same incivility, the same propensity to put counting partisan coup over serving the common good during the Bush years.

Indeed, it is remarkable how quickly we went from comparisons of Bush to Hitler, and dire warnings about our descent into right-wing fascism, to comparisons of Obama to Hitler, and dire warnings about our descent into left-wing socialism. Hatred and fear, apparently, can turn on a dime. As one author has aptly noted, "[i]f you only object to the president of your party being compared to Hitler, then you're part of the problem."[89]

More broadly, globally, our modern world is marked by the rise of intolerant extremism in various guises and forms. As Prime Minister Razak of Malaysia noted in remarks to the United Nations, "we have inadvertently allowed the ugly voices of the periphery to drown out the many voices of reason and common sense."[90] This is as true here at home as it is abroad in distant lands.

Given the fact that these proclivities are present across the political spectrum, they must speak to broader problems within our culture, within us. This begs the question - what is it that we are afraid of? Why are we, at this moment in our history, so lacking in hope and faith in the future? Why are we so ready to believe the very worst about each other?

These questions call for much further reflection, but I have some initial thoughts. I think it goes back to the depersonalization, the atomization of the individual, that is the hallmark of modernity. That and anomie. We feel alone, beset by forces more powerful than ourselves, lost in a trackless waste unmarked by any path. We sense danger approaching. And we are most fearful of the unknown when we are alone. Finally, we must also admit that many among us have become, in a political and economic sense, extremely selfish and beset by resentments.

As a result, we become desperate for the semblance of any solution, for some safe harbor. Thus, we flee from "the desert of the real" to the illusive comfort of a false certainty. We long for a world marked by good guys and bad guys, heroes and villains, and a clear narrative, a simple story line that we can take hold of and use to orient ourselves and make sense of the confusing static and noise that surrounds us. The problem here is that the Tea Party narrative, while perhaps psychologically comforting, is not a safe harbor. It is, in fact, a trap. The success of the Tea Party is not a transformative event promising a better tomorrow but rather a step toward disaster.

A public discourse dominated by an "us versus them," litmus test- oriented storyline focused on ideological purity that views politics as a zero-sum game and demonizes opponents, cannot advance the common good. It is not conducive to fostering the type of open and honest debate we need in order to find solutions to the problems facing us. It is not conducive to building coalitions, and to working together. It inflames divisions, and expands the crevices forming in society separating us from each other.

As a nation, our only hope is to cast off fear and to face reality, the world as it is, with courage and conviction. I am convinced that most of us want a future in which we, and our children and grandchildren, can reach our full potential as human beings. One in which, as much as is practically possible, opportunity and prosperity are open to all. One unmarked by grave inequalities in the distribution of wealth and resources. One in which essential human rights are recognized and respected. One conducive both to the development of our intellects and to the formation of our consciences.

The key to avoiding a dystopian future is *agape*. Love speaks to dignity. It speaks to solidarity. It speaks to the common good. It speaks to how we interact with one another, especially when we disagree. It is a bridge across whatever chasms divide us. It is an equalizer, a leveler of distinctions among us. It binds us together in the common project of securing a better future. It replaces atomization with brotherhood, anomie with purpose and meaning. Fear fuels anger and resentment but love is the kindling for hope. It is the invitation to something better. Our love for each other is the key to everything.

It is agape then, that, to paraphrase Prime Minister Razak, "will save us from sinking into the abyss of despair and depravation."[91] It is agape that holds within itself the opportunity to "bring hope and restore dignity for all."[92]

The problems we face are profound, and the perils are real. The Psalmist says that when we were children we spoke as children - but now we are at childhood's end, and so we must put away the things of our youth in order to go forward, and thrive. It is impossible to safely navigate the precipice of the present if we are at each other's throats. Therefore, there can be no more us versus them; there must rather be all of us together. Avoiding a dystopian tomorrow is the life's work of our generation - it is our common project. And everything turns on our love for one another - that is the great truth that I have enough courage still to say.

--

[88] Scarborough, Joe. (Nov. 30, 2010). "Joe Scarborough tells GOP to man up and confront Sarah Palin." Politico.

[89] Avlon, John. (April 1, 2010). "Getting Hit with the Hitler Card." The Daily Beast.

[90] Fallows, James. (Sept. 28, 2010). "A 'Global Movement of Moderates': Speech of a Muslim Prime Minister." The Atlantic Monthly.

[91] Id.

[92] Id.

14.
Restore the
Constitution?

"Restore the Constitution!" It's a cry, in various iterations, that one commonly hears from the Tea Party. There have been "Restore the Constitution" rallies calling for "restoring the rule of law," there are "Restore the Constitution" petitions circulating online, and there are "Restore the Constitution" blog sites. Politically, the Tea Party movement takes great pains to portray itself as a defender of the Constitution, keeping faith with the original intent of the Founding Fathers.

This is ironic. A deeper examination of positions commonly held by the Tea Party, particularly regarding the scope of the 10th Amendment, the repeal or modification of the 14th, 16th, and 17th Amendments, and the support for various nullification proposals, reflects a hostility to aspects of the Constitution as well as opposition to well-established principles in our Constitutional jurisprudence.

In the end, the vision of our Constitution expressed by the Tea Party movement is often fundamentally at odds with that of many of our leading Founders, including Washington, Adams, Hamilton, Jay, Marshall, and Madison (prior to his 1791 break with Hamilton).

A telling omission: The Tea Party and the 10th Amendment

The 10th Amendment features prominently in the Constitutionalism of the Tea Party. It provides that: "The powers not delegated to the United States by the Constitution, nor prohibited by it to the States, are reserved to the States respectively, or to the people." To the Tea Party, the 10th Amendment is a forgotten (or ignored) restriction limiting the powers of the federal government to those explicitly enumerated in the Constitution.

Instead, what is actually ignored is the history of the 10th Amendment. During the debates in Congress over what ultimately became the Bill of Rights, James Madison successfully defeated a motion to add the word "expressly" - as in "the powers not expressly delegated" - to the 10th Amendment, because, in his words, "it [is] impossible to confine a Government to the exercise of express powers; there must necessarily be admitted powers by implication."[93] Ignoring Madison's logic, many in the Tea Party would write the word "expressly" back into the 10th Amendment though its narrow interpretation.

The Tea Party's vision of the 10th Amendment also ignores the jurisprudential legacy of one of our earliest, and most consequential, Chief Justices - John Marshall. According to Chris Satullo of WHYY in Delaware, "John Marshall, as much as any man save for the great James Madison, determined what our founding charter really meant, and did so in ways that enabled the American experiment to thrive."[94] In this regard, note that "thriving" is inextricably intertwined with a limited, but vigorous and capable, federal government.

According to Satullo, Marshall fundamentally:

> "[I]nterpreted the Constitution in a way opposite to the Tea Partiers and libertarians who now cite the 10th Amendment as cause to roll back the clock to 1850.
>
> Marshall led the Supreme Court over 34 years, deciding the key cases that established the court as an equal branch and shaped the role of the federal government.
>
> One of those cases is McCulloch v. Maryland. Apparently, the Tea Partiers now carrying on about the 10th Amendment never heard of McCulloch or think it wrongly decided…"
>
> Tea Partiers today insist, following their hero Jefferson (no fan of the Constitution), that this clause limits Congress and the President only to those powers specifically named. They would have our leaders hamstrung in the face of any event not anticipated in 1787. They would declare illegal most of modern government, from the Tennessee Valley Authority to Social Security to the EPA.
>
> But Marshall decided McCulloch, the great test of this question, in precisely the opposite way, establish-

ing that the federal government has implicit powers to 'ensure the general welfare'..."[95]

In the end, as one legal scholar has concluded, the Tea Party's narrow reading of the 10th Amendment "is without support in [its] legislative history or [in] Supreme Court" precedent.[96]

"Constitutional graffiti"

At the same time, some Congressional Republicans have been busy proposing numerous Constitutional edits and fixes. These include: repeal of the 17th Amendment (ending the direct election of Senators), amending the 14th Amendment (to end birthright citizenship), a prohibition on government ownership of private corporate stock, a "Parental Rights Amendment," various proposed term-limits amendments, an amendment prohibiting flag burning, various balanced-budget amendments, a national prohibition on gay marriage, an amendment requiring a super-majority vote for any tax increases, and an amendment restricting the President's authority to negotiate treaties. Reaching back to the antebellum "nullification" debates, Rep. Eric Cantor (R-VA), has even called for a "Repeal Amendment" which would provide for the nullification of federal laws by a two-thirds majority of the states, and there have been other calls for "nullification" as well.

In the 2010 election campaign, other candidates identified with the Tea Party weighed in offering their own Constitutional tweaks. For example, Joe Miller in Alaska announced that unemployment benefits were unconstitutional (despite the fact that he formerly received them), while Rand Paul said the same thing about aspects of the Civil Rights Act of 1964. Sharron Angle (along with

Glenn Beck) called for the repeal of the 16th Amendment (which established the federal income tax).

The movements to repeal or amend the 14th, 16th, and 17th Amendments, warrant further analysis as they illuminate the populist, libertarian assault on the Constitution and federal authority presently underway.

The radical Right has become the political home of modern nativism. This finds expression in calls for the modification of the 14th Amendment to eliminate birthright citizenship. The 14th Amendment is a legacy of the Civil War and Reconstruction. It plainly states, "All persons born or naturalized in the United States and subject to the jurisdiction thereof, are citizens of the United States and of the State wherein they reside." Therefore, anyone born in the United States is a citizen, and entitled to the equal protection of the law. Today, some in the Tea Party would strike from the Constitution one of the most seminal statements elucidating the concept of human freedom ever written in the history of the world. The movement to amend the 14th Amendment is an ominous harbinger of other dangers ahead.

Calls for the repeal of the 16th Amendment are particularly reckless and irresponsible. The 16th Amendment, ratified in 1913, gives Congress the "power to lay and collect taxes on incomes, from whatever source derived . . . ." The power to tax, however, was not a 20th Century addition to the Constitution- Article I, Section 8 vests Congress with the "[p]ower to lay and collect Taxes, Duties, Imposts and Excises, to pay the Debts and provide for the common Defence and general Welfare of the United States . . ." Given this clear language, one might ask, why was the 16th Amendment needed? The answer is simple- it was necessary in order to reverse a Supreme Court decision, *Pollock v. Farmers' Loan & Trust Co.*, holding that the federal income tax was unconstitutional. The Pollock case is significant in that the Court broke with its own prior precedent affirming the constitutionality of the federal income tax, such as *Springer v. United States* (an 1889 case upholding the Constitutionality of a federal income tax), and ignored the clear language of Article I, Section 8.

While the level of the federal income tax and its structure is open to debate, there can be no dispute that it was an essential element in the creation of a stronger America. And that was a necessary predicate to America's world-saving role in the 20th Century when the United States defended liberty across the globe from both the specter of Nazism and from Communist tyranny. Those who would gut our national power, like Glenn Beck and Sharron Angle, either imagine that similar dangers will never arise in the future, or worse, simply do not care.

The 17th Amendment provides for the direct election of United States Senators. Under the original Constitution, they were appointed directly by state legislatures. Like the 16th Amendment, it was also ratified in 1913. Astonishingly, its repeal has become a favorite cause of Tea Party candidates across America. For example, speaking in July, Rep. Paul Broun (R-GA) informed a Tea Party crowd that the adoption of the 16th and 17th Amendments began the "process of socializing America," and called for both should be repealed. Sen. Mike Lee (R-Utah), Rep. Jeff Landry (R-LA), and Rep. Raul Labrador (R-ID) also expressed support for repealing the 17th Amendment during the election campaign.

The direct election of Senators by the people might sound

innocuous, but in the opinion of the Tea Party, its ratification "dealt a blow to the Framers' vision of the Constitution from which we have yet to recover."[97] In the view of the Tea Party, repealing it would enhance "states' rights." This puts the Tea Party in the awkward position of arguing that democracy isn't a good thing. It also illuminates the real motivation in play- weakening the federal government, weakening the Union, and empowering State governments - which is separate and distinct from empowering citizens. To illustrate this point, consider: is it better to have United States Senators representing your *state legislature*, or representing *you*?

An objective observer would call all of this "re-writing," not "restoring." And there is no remotely comparable activity occuring on the political left. As one author has noted, "the self-proclaimed party of conservatism has become a constitutional graffiti movement."[98]

Our modern Anti-Federalists

In its attempt to portray itself as the defender of the Constitution, the Tea Party appropriates the legacy of the Founding Fathers. However, the Federalist Papers, and the actions of Washington, Hamilton, Adams, and Marshall while in office reflect a rather different view of federalism and the nature of the Constitutional compact. That is not surprising. They knew that the Constitution created a strong national government - indeed, that was the point of the entire process of calling the Constitutional convention in Philadelphia in the first place. Such a vision is fundamentally at odds with reading the 10th Amendment as a veritable straight jacket restricting national power, with support for Cantor's Repeal Amendment and state "nullification" laws, or with calls for the repeal of the 16th

Amendment.

In their dogmatic opposition to a strong central governing authority, the Tea Party actually voices views similar to those expressed by opponents of the Constitution during the ratification debates. They are the modern heirs of the Anti-Federalists, and not of the Founders. And that is very problematic, because if the Anti-Federalists had prevailed in the early years of the Republic, it is unlikely America would have grown into the prosperous, free, powerful, and united nation spanning an entire continent that it ultimately became. Indeed, it is quite possible it might not have survived at all.

These facts frame what the Tea Party means by "Restore the Constitution." They are not referring to the document we have lived with for the past two hundred years - the one that helped our nation achieve hitherto unprecedented levels of prosperity and freedom. And, however loudly they may say they love the Constitution and the Founders, the truth is that they would amend or repeal crucial elements of it, in effect jettisoning more than two centuries' of jurisprudence, and redefining federalism in a way that reverses the outcome of the Constitutional ratification debates and even of the Civil War.

In the end, I do not think that it is the Constitution that the Tea Party really wants to restore; I think it is the Articles of Confederation.

--

[93] Annals of Congress. The Debates and Proceedings in the Congress of the United States. "History of Congress." 42 vols. Washington, D.C.: Gales & Seaton, 1834—56. Retrieved from: http://press-pubs.uchicago.edu/founders/documents/amendXs6.html

[94] Satullo, Chris. (Oct. 3, 2010). "Tea Party, meet John Marshall." WHYY. Retrieved from: http://whyy.org/cms/news/centersquare/2010/10/03/tea-party-meet-john-marshall/47223

[95] Id.

[96] Becker, Joseph D. (April 26, 2010). "Tea party civics." The National Law Journal.

[97] Zywicki, Todd. (Nov. 15, 2010). "Repeal the Seventeenth Amendment." National Review.

[98] Schlesinger, Robert. (Sept. 8, 2010). "The GOP, Tea Party Declare War on Constitution." U.S. News & World Report.

15.

The Party of Lincoln Needs to Look in the Mirror

In the spring of 2011, a tape of NPR's head fundraiser, Ron Schiller, making remarks critical of the GOP and the Tea Party surfaced. In the tape, Schiller referred to the Republican Party as "anti-intellectual" and described the Tea Party as "racist," "Islamophobic," and "xenophobic." He went on to opine that "Jews" control America's major newspapers.

Schiller's bizarre and conspiratorial anti-Semitic remarks are disturbing and offensive. His remarks about the GOP and the Tea Party, though, warrant further analysis for a simple reason: they are perceptions widely shared in our society.

Conservatives reacted to Schiller's comments with anger.

In their eyes, it was just one more example of a liberal establishment standing ever ready to portray Republicans and conservatives as ignorant racists and bigots.

That reaction was a mistake. In truth, Schiller created an opportunity for discussion and critical self-analysis, for an honest dialog about race, religion, and science within the Republican Party. This was an opportunity, not for anger, but for self-examination. Simply put, it's time for the Party of Lincoln to take a good look in the mirror.

Although conservatives are quick to dismiss Schiller's remarks, there is ample evidence available that would lead reasonable people to such conclusions. One can point to examples such as Sharron Angle's 2010 anti-immigrant campaign television ads,[99] Renee Ellmer's overtly Islamophobic "Ground Zero" ad,[100] Sen. Rand Paul's remarks about the alleged unconstitutionality of portions of the Civil Rights Act of 1964, the career and associations of Arizona State Senator Russell Pearce (the man who sponsored Arizona's infamous SB 1070), and Kansas State Representative Virgil Peck's recent suggestion that illegal immigrants should be hunted and shot like feral swine.[101]

And this is just the tip of the iceberg.

According to a February, 2012 survey by Public Policy Polling ("PPP"), 51% of likely Republican primary voters believe President Obama was born in a foreign country. Some 21% are "not sure."[102] Other data suggests that a significant percentage believe the President is secretly a Muslim. Even more troublingly, a separate April, 2011 PPP poll found that 46% of Mississippi Republicans believe that interracial marriage should be a crime while a substantial group, 12%, indicated that they are "not sure."[103]

And then there are the e-mails. Nationally, Republican staffers[104] and local party officials[105] have made headlines forwarding racist e-mails about the President to friends and colleagues. And lest we forget, there is also the case of Audra Shay, who was elected Chair of the national Young Republicans despite the fact that she had replied "You tell em Eric! Lol," to a friend's Facebook comment that said: "Obama Bin Lauden [sic] is the new terrorist... Muslim is on there side [sic]... need to take this country back from all of these mad coons... and illegals."[106]

Nor is the depth, breadth, and intensity of Tea Party rage explicable without reference to the presence of an African American, with a foreign sounding name, in the White House.

The practical electoral implications of this mindless fear and hate were brought home to me on a trip to D.C. with representatives of *Esperanza*, a national faith-based Hispanic organization. One pastor spoke of a young man in his congregation - a young, conservative, Christian man - who was deeply torn over his choices in the 2008 Presidential election. In the end, he voted for Obama because, as he said, "I can't be in a Party that hates me." I don't blame him.

And, as a consequence, in a United States growing increasingly diverse, the GOP is devolving into an ethnic/regional party. Worse, it will be a minority ethnic party incapable of winning national elections. Remember, today Caucasians, the group from which the GOP draws the vast majority of its support, make up less than half - 49.3% - of children under 3 years of age. According to U.S. census projections, by 2019, Caucasians will make up less than half of Americans aged 18 and under.[107]

As Harold Meyerson has observed, "[w]hat these numbers mean is simply that the Republicans have an existential problem. As America becomes increasingly multiracial, the Republicans have elected to become increasingly white."[108]

A more diverse, majority-minority America is inevitable - the GOP, and conservatives in general, need to adjust and adapt to this reality if they want to remain relevant over the long-term. Texas, for example, will, in a few Presidential election cycles, probably be solidly blue, if current voting patterns there continue. A future GOP that serves as a bastion for angry, resentful and embittered, "white minority politics" would be an unmitigated disaster for our nation and for the health of our democracy.[109]

Thankfully, however, a path out of the wilderness has already been charted out for us. As Tim Mak noted in June 2010 on FrumForum, Canada's Conservative Party has made winning the immigrant and minority vote a top priority.[110] In Canada, Conservatives were facing a "structural political problem"- the growth of minority communities among which the Conservative Party performed poorly threatened to render it "uncompetitive over the long term." Facing negative public perceptions among minority voters, Canada's Conservatives executed a comprehensive outreach plan featuring sustained attention and engagement aimed at overcoming barriers to understanding. As an initial matter, the Party looked for niche issues that had appeal to key communities. Attention to these issues helped to build trust and made the Conservative Party relevant in a way it had not been before as it used these "door openers" to begin a conversation with minority voters.

The fruits of this approach have been impressive- the Conservative Party has registered significant electoral gains.

Like Canada's Conservatives, the GOP is facing a structural political problem - its most dependable voters constitute a declining share of the American electorate in a rapidly diversifying nation. Like Canada's Conservatives, Republicans face prevalent negative perceptions within minority communities that act as barriers to engagement on important issues.

Today, it is essential that Republicans of good will confront the racists, the xenophobes, and the anti-intellectual elements in our midst while, at the same time, beginning a conversation with immigrant and minority communities. In doing so, we are keeping faith with the best traditions of our Party, and preserving an alternate, more welcoming and inclusive vision of political conservatism in America, one in which Conservative is not synonymous with Confederate.

--

[99] SharronAngle. (Oct. 25, 2010). "The Wave." YouTube. Retrieved from: http://www.youtube.com/watch?v=tIkNAA2y4I4&feature=player_embedded

[100] ReneeforCongress. (Sept. 21, 2010). "No Mosque at Ground Zero." YouTube. Retrieved from: http://www.youtube.com/watch?v=0QvKOdiyFaw

[101] KCTV 5 News. (Mar. 15, 2011). "Kansas Rep. Suggests Shooting Illegal Immigrants Like Hogs."

[102] Schlesinger, Robert. (Feb. 16, 2011). "Poll: Birthers Now Make Up a Majority of Republican Primary Voters." U.S. News & World Report.

[103] Public Policy Polling. (April 7, 2011). "Barbour, Bryant lead in Mississippi." Retrieved from: http://publicpolicypolling.blogspot.com/2011/04/barbour-bryant-lead-in-mississippi.html

[104] Pareene. (Jun. 15, 2009) "Today's 'Racist Email From a Republican Staffer.'" Gawker. Retrieved from: http://gawker.com/#!5291679/todays-racist-email-from-a-republican-staffer

[105] Murphy, Logan. (Oct. 31, 2008). "FL GOP Chair Sends Out Racist E-mail: Beware of the Car Loads of Blacks." Crooks and Liars. Retrieved from: http://crooksandliars.com/logan-murphy/fl-gop-chair-sends-out-racist-e-mail-

[106] Rowe, Michael. (July 12, 2009). "Audra Shay and the New Ice Age of Young Republicans." Huffington Post. Retrieved from: http://www.huffingtonpost.com/michael-rowe/the-new-ice-age-of-the-yo_b_230125.html

[107] Tavernise, Sabrina. (April 6, 2011). "Numbers of Children of Whites Falling Fast." The New York Times.

[108] Meyerson, Harold. (Mar. 3, 2011). "Republicans fighting demographic change." The Washington Post.

[109] Indeed, given the fact that the nation will be increasingly divided between an older, predominantly white, population and a younger, far more ethnically and racially diverse one, it may also serve to exacerbate intergeneration conflicts over the division of resources and public policy priorities. Navigating the transition to a "majority minority" future safely, and in a way that serves the common good, is one of the greatest political challenges facing our nation today. It cries out for forward-looking, responsible, leadership.

[110] Mak, Tim. (June 7, 2010). "How Canada's Conservatives Won The Immigrant Vote." FrumForum. Retrieved from: http://www.frumforum.com/how-canadas-conservatives-won-the-immigrant-vote

16.

Soda Doesn't Kill You, But Tobacco Parties Will

"The political parties are like Coke and Pepsi." If I have heard that expression once, I've heard it a thousand times.

I don't think it's an apt analogy though. It certainly serves to illustrate the limited range of political choices available to us - two products that are fundamentally similar and differ, principally, in aesthetic details and points of emphasis. But soda is a relatively benign product. Sure, we all know it isn't nutritious, and that consuming too much of it will damage your teeth, but it's not an inherently dangerous beverage.

Are our political parties today really analogous to soda? I think not.

The Democrats and Republicans are not Coke and Pepsi, and they are not selling soda. Today, they have become more like Philip Morris and R.J. Reynolds. And what they are pitching is destroying our nation.

Over the past 30 years, America has witnessed an unprecedented concentration of wealth at the very top. This small group, the top 1%, are the primary beneficiaries of the economic expansion that has occurred over the past three decades. They have grown fabulously rich. We can call this process "the Great Divergence." They have separated themselves, in economic terms, from you, and me, and everyone else, by several orders of magnitude.[111]

The Great Divergence has been, demonstrably, unhealthy for the nation. And as Joseph E. Stiglitz has observed, "growing inequality is the flip side of something else: shrinking opportunity.... America's inequality distorts our society in every conceivable way."[112] The "Great Divergence" has coincided with the gutting of our manufacturing base, and the hollowing out of the middle class. During this period, we've gone from being a nation that makes things, to a nation that merely consumes them. Moreover, the emergence of the super-rich is inextricably entwined with the rise of celebrity culture and consumerism. And this process, the movement from a production to a consumption ethic, isn't value neutral.

In America, the free market does not exist to advance social justice, or further the common good. It has become an end unto itself. In our society everything - human beings, the environment, literally everything - has been commodified and objectified. As a culture, we have adopted a selfish form of Social Darwinism - a survival-of-the-fittest approach to economics and, increasingly, to public policy.

Success, winning, has become the only warrant we recognize. To illustrate this point, simply consider the similarities between the values and ethics displayed on "Survivor" and those of the top executives in the financial industry whose rapacious greed brought on the global financial crisis. In "Survivor," winning requires lying, cheating, ignoring the rights of others. Other people are not friends, they are objects to use, and suckers to be played and manipulated. As Chris Hedges has noted, the economic ethic of the market today is indistinguishable from that depicted on "Survivor" - win at all costs. Win by any means necessary. And, like the winner of "Survivor," we watched our financial sector executives walk off the stage keeping their millions in bloated compensation and bonuses. They just don't get a reunion show.

Meanwhile, the middle class has sunk into debt in an, ultimately vain, effort to keep up with the mega-rich Joneses. And, this is not surprising. The lifestyles of the super-rich are on full public display, and we are constantly tempted to emulate them. We have been sold a Great Lie - that the act of consuming, and the possession of material things can give our lives purpose and meaning. But no house, or car, or shoes, or purse, ever fills the void inside us and, like addicts, we are soon back out on the streets looking for the next hit. The advertising we are bombarded with will always create new insecurities and anxieties to fill and new envies to feed - after all, it has to keep us buying. Slowly, inexorably, we have allowed this process to bankrupt ourselves and our nation.

Inevitably, great concentrations of wealth engender great concentrations of power. It is naïve to believe otherwise. The Great Divergence - which is continuing even today in the midst of the current crisis - is not in the best interests of our nation. Today, we are flirting with the permanent empowerment of an oligarchic class that will have total control of the media, the entertainment industry, the economy, and the government.

And, neither political party will do anything to end the oligarchs' lucky run at the public craps table - a lucky run totally dependent on the continuation of a socially Darwinian market ethic, consumerism, and our culture of consumption. This is why neither party puts forth proposals for systemic reform that would fundamentally threaten or reverse the Great Divergence and empower the middle class. Despite the hyper-partisanship, and despite the heated rhetoric that characterizes our politics, very little, in terms of *deeds,* separates our two parties when it comes to how they treat the super-rich, and the Great Divergence. A cynic might rightly wonder whether the rhetoric isn't used to mask the absence of real choice in the system.

But, our choices are not limited to the cold, cruel, and impersonal ethic of the unrestricted, unregulated free market and the bankrupt policies of statist collectivism. The worst excesses of the market can be mitigated without impairing its dynamic and creative forces. If that were to happen, then its power could be made to serve the common good, and to advance justice rather than inequality.

However, at this juncture, expecting either party to proffer such a solution is akin to expecting Philip Morris and R.J. Reynolds to have, on their own, decided to warn us all of the dangers of smoking.

Is it possible to reform the existing parties internally? If so, can it be done in time? Can one, or both, be transformed into an agent of constructive change? What needs to be done to effectuate this? Is this type of reform preferable to setting up a new political structure? More importantly, can the necessary alliances between reform elements on the right and left be forged across the ideological chasm? How can we foster such a process?

Those are the urgent questions all people of good will should be considering right now. Because if we do nothing, our two tobacco parties are going to kill this nation.

--

[111] For more on "the Great Divergence," see Noah, Timothy. (Sep. 3, 2010). "The United States of Inequality: Introducing the Great Divergence." Slate. Retrieved from: http://www.slate.com/id/2266025/entry/2266026

[112] Stiglitz, Joseph E. (May, 2011). "Of the 1%, by the 1%, for the 1%." Vanity Fair.

17.

It's a Jungle Out There: Income Inequality, Taxation, and Economic Justice

For the past three decades, the super-rich, a group we can define as the top 1% of wage earners in the United States, have reaped a disproportionate share of the economic benefits in this nation while paying a declining percentage of their income in taxes. They have been the primary beneficiaries of the tremendous economic expansion that has occurred over this period. Today, at a time of fiscal and economic crisis, as the core federal programs underpinning the social contract come under threat, those who have gained the most from the boom would leave the rest of us to bear the burden of the bust.

Vanderbilt, Rockefeller, Carnegie - these names conjure images of America's "Gilded Age" - a time of oligarchic capitalism prior to the Great Depression and Roosevelt's

"New Deal." Amazingly, today, America has a greater disparity in income and wealth distribution than it had during the early 20th Century. For example, in 1915, the top 1% in America earned roughly 15 to 18% of the nation's income. Today, they account for a quarter of it.[113]

Writing in *Slate*, Timothy Noah has observed that:

> "Income inequality in the United States has not worsened steadily since 1915. It dropped a bit in the late teens, then started climbing again in the 1920s, reaching its peak just before the 1929 crash. The trend then reversed itself. Incomes started to become more equal in the 1930s and then became dramatically more equal in the 1940s. Income distribution remained roughly stable through the postwar economic boom of the 1950s and 1960s. Economic historians Claudia Goldin and Robert Margo have termed this midcentury era the "Great Compression." The deep nostalgia for that period felt by the World War II generation—the era of Life magazine and the bowling league—reflects something more than mere sentimentality. Assuming you were white, not of draft age, and Christian, there probably was no better time to belong to America's middle class... The Great Compression ended in the 1970s. Wages stagnated, inflation raged, and by the decade's end, income inequality had started to rise. Income inequality grew through the 1980s, slackened briefly at the end of the 1990s, and then resumed with a vengeance in the aughts.

> From the mid-1970's to today, the top 1% have seen a precipitous rise in their incomes at a time when, for most Americans, wages have remained relatively

flat. The growth in incomes among the wealthy has also coincided with a period of increasing corporate profits."[114]

A few statistics will demonstrate the remarkable extent of the windfall reaped by the super-rich over the past three decades. According to economist Paul Krugman, the top 1% account for over 80% of the total increases to income during the 25-year period from 1980 to 2005. Today, the top 1% annually account for a quarter of the nation's earned income, and they control roughly 40% of America's wealth.

At the same time, massive productivity increases during this period did not lead to wage increases for American workers. Indeed, Americans "in the middle have actually seen their incomes fall" over the past decade. "For men with only high-school degrees, the decline has been precipitous—12 percent in the last quarter-century alone."[115] The conclusion is inescapable - the lion's share of the wealth generated during the boom years was captured by a remarkably small segment of our society.

As a result, today, income and wealth distribution in the United States is more unequal than in many nations in Latin America.

As Timothy Noah noted, the 1950's and 1960's represent a mythic "golden age" for middle class America- if you were white and a male. 1965 is, roughly, at the mid point of that era- the pinnacle of egalitarian, "middle class" capitalism. In 1965, the effective tax rate on individuals earning the equivalent of $1 million in income was a whopping 55.2%. By the beginning of the Reagan administration, this number had fallen to 47.7%. In 2000, before the enactment of the Bush tax cuts, the number had fallen further to 36.4%. After the Bush tax cuts, in 2010, the number was 32.4%.[116]

This discussion of effective tax rates also masks the effect of readily-available loopholes and deductions on income taxes paid by the most wealthy individuals in our society. For example, according to an April, 2011 article by Dave Gilson in Mother Jones, the average income among the 400 taxpayers with the highest annual incomes in America has increased by 329% from 1992 to 2007. Meanwhile, their average effective tax rate dropped by 32%.[117]

Thus, the great concentration of wealth among the super-rich over the past three decades has coincided with a remarkable decrease in their rate of federal taxation.

The "Great Divergence" has also coincided with a marked increase in the influence wielded by large corporations in Washington, D.C. In particular, corporations now spend billions of dollars every year lobbying elected officials and influencing political campaigns. This is something new in our politics and its' growth correlates, almost precisely, to the beginning of the "Great Divergence" in the 1970's.

Unfortunately, the Supreme Court's recent decision in *Citizens United* will only serve to accelerate this process.

The growing income disparity in America has profound political, economic, and cultural implications for our society. Again, to quote Noah:

> "[I]ncome inequality is a topic of huge importance to American society and therefore a subject of large and growing interest to a host of economists, politi-

cal scientists, and other wonky types. Except for a few Libertarian outliers (whose views we'll examine later), these experts agree that the country's growing income inequality is deeply worrying. Even Alan Greenspan, the former Federal Reserve Board chairman and onetime Ayn Rand acolyte, has registered concern. 'This is not the type of thing which a democratic society—a capitalist democratic society—can really accept without addressing,' Greenspan said in 2005."

Or, as Joseph E. Stiglitz put it in *Vanity Fair*: "An economy in which most citizens are doing worse year after year—an economy like America's—is not likely to do well over the long haul."[118]

In addition, a society marked by gross, and growing, inequalities of wealth is one that will, inevitably, neglect the commons:

> "The more divided a society becomes in terms of wealth, the more reluctant the wealthy become to spend money on common needs. The rich don't need to rely on government for parks or education or medical care or personal security—they can buy all these things for themselves. In the process, they become more distant from ordinary people, losing whatever empathy they may once have had. They also worry about strong government—one that could use its powers to adjust the balance, take some of their wealth, and invest it for the common good."

At the core of the problem, I think, is our elevation of the unrestricted, unregulated, "free" market to divine status. The market no longer serves as a means to an end, it has become an end unto itself. We seem to have forgotten that the economy, like all human activity, has a moral component, and that it "should serve people, not the other way around."[119]

In the end, the foundation of the "Great Divergence" is to be found in failures in commutative and distributive justice within our society. For a growing percentage of Americans, hard work and honest labor is no longer rewarded with fair wages and benefits, nor any type of meaningful job security. Nor is the outcome of allocations of wealth and power in our society "fair" in any sense that does not make a mockery of the word. Indeed, our failures in commutative and distributive justice will only be exacerbated by proposals to tear up the social contract, or eviscerate the power of the federal government, particularly if such measures coincide with further tax reductions on the top 1% and corporations.

The "Great Divergence" is, in other words, ultimately the product of a moral and ethical failure on the part of our society. The market will not produce justice and equity on its own and, left to its own devices, can be as destructive of human dignity and the common good as the old communist command economies. This is a point that Pope Benedict XVI has recognized:

> "Both capitalism and Marxism promised to point out the path for the creation of just structures, and they declared that these, once established, would function by themselves... And this ideological promise has been proved false. The facts have clearly demonstrated it. The Marxist system, where it found its way into government, not only left a sad heritage of economic and ecological destruction, but also a painful oppres-

sion of souls. And we can also see the same thing happening in the West, where the distance between rich and poor is growing constantly, and giving rise to a worrying degradation of personal dignity…"

As a result, we now stand on the cusp of a new Gilded Age, one marked by growing inequalities in wealth, income, and opportunity, in which business and government are increasingly dominated and controlled by an oligarchic class. Actually, on second thought, "Gilded Age" isn't an apt description. The Rockefellers and Vanderbilts, after all, had a well-developed sense of noblesse oblige that is totally alien to many of our oligarchs today. Rather then a new Gilded Age, our present situation is perhaps better described as a descent into Hobbes' Jungle, an economic version of the war of all, against all.

And like any Jungle, this one cries out for a Leviathan. Here, that can only be the federal government. While it is true, to paraphrase Pope Benedict XVI, that the State can never love you, it can, consistent with the principle of subsidiarity, be a vehicle for public policies that promote social and economic justice.[120] It can accomplish this, in part, through its tax and regulatory policies.

At a time when Congress is considering major cuts to critical entitlement programs, such as Medicare, in the name of fiscal austerity, it is necessary and appropriate that we have an open and honest discussion about the distribution of the burdens created by fiscal retrenching.

It is also time to have an open and honest discussion about our collective refusal to pay for the services we expect government to provide. In the end, the federal budget deficit isn't going to be eliminated through budget cuts alone, nor will the best interests of our society be served by the elimination of the social safety net.

It's time to look at expenditures *and* revenues. Simply put - the super-rich, and the large corporations they control, can pay a little more.[121]

As such, it's time to seriously consider raising the personal income tax rates on the top 1% (or, at the very least, on the top decile of the top 1%) and, perhaps, returning them to the levels of the mid to early 1990's as well as increasing the effective corporate tax rates. While not a total solution, such measures would ensure a more equitable distribution of burdens and benefits within our economic system. It would be a first, tentative step, in the right direction.

At the same time, although we readily recognize the detrimental effects of too much regulation on the creative and dynamic forces of the market, we have now seen, in the financial crisis, the perils of the other extreme - too little regulation. It's incumbent on us to strike a better balance.[122]

This is *not* a call to "soak the rich" or an appeal to class warfare. It *is* a reminder that economic and political systems must serve the *common good* and that they do not exist to further the interests of an entrenched oligarchic class at the expense of the rest of us.

Realistically, standing alone, increasing taxes on the wealthy or corporations will not solve the budgetary problems facing the federal government - programmatic cuts are coming, too. However, it is critical that the looming burdens and sacrifices be distributed fairly. It is legitimate to expect that those that reaped the lion's share of the benefits of our economic expansion will share, at least as much, in the pain caused by the impact of the economic crash.

And looking a bit further down the road, we must address the systemic causes that have led to the "Great Divergence," and redress the political balance between the power of the super-rich, and the middle and working classes, if we want our economy, and our democracy, to thrive.

--

[113] Noah, Timothy. (Sep. 3, 2010). "The United States of Inequality: Introducing the Great Divergence." Slate. Retrieved from: http://www.slate.com/id/2266025/entry/2266026

[114] Id.

[115] Stiglitz, Joseph E. (May, 2011). "Of the 1%, by the 1%, for the 1%." Vanity Fair.

[116] Gilson, Dave and Perot, Carolyn. (March/April 2011). "It's the Inequality, Stupid." Mother Jones.

[117] Gilson, Dave. (April 18, 2011). "Only little people pay taxes." Mother Jones.

[118] Stiglitz, "Of the 1%, by the 1%, for the 1%."

[119] Economic Justice For All. US Catholic Bishops (NCCB), 1986.

[120] See: "God is Love: Encyclical Letter of Pope Benedict XVI"

[121] Although America has one of the highest top marginal corporate tax rates in the world, the effective tax rate paid by our biggest corporations is much lower due to the existence of numerous loopholes and deductions. For my own part, I would lower the top marginal rate while, at the same time, raising the effective rate through the rationalization and simplification of the tax code. In a way, placing this burden on business makes sense- it eliminates the windfall profits realized

by the elimination of pensions, the curtailment of benefits, and the outsourcing of many jobs overseas, in the private sector over the past several decades. Dixon, Kim. (April 17, 2011). "Are U.S. companies drowning in taxes or artful dodgers?" MSNBC. Retrieved from: http://www.msnbc.msn.com/id/42595784/ns/business-tax_tactics/

[122] In the long-term, the worst excesses of the market might be ameliorated without impairing its creative forces through the adoption of a "communitarian democratic capitalism" that provides a more "humane and ethical alternative" to the impersonal coldness, cruelty, and injustice of the unregulated market. See Oliver F. Williams, C.S.C., "Catholic Social Teaching: A Communitarian Democratic Capitalism for the New World Order," Journal of Business Ethics, Vol. 12, No. 12, Dec. 1993.

18.

Ryan, Rand, and the Objectivist Budget

On April 15, 2011, four members of the House Republican Caucus voted against Congressman Paul Ryan's budgetary "Path to Prosperity."

Had I been there and had the opportunity to do so, I would have proudly been among their number.

There's a simple reason for this: Paul Ryan is an "[Ayn] Rand nut."[123] His proposal isn't a path to prosperity or fiscal sanity, it's a projection of an Objectivist vision for our society, our nation, and its future. And that's a dark path we'd do well to avoid.

I'm not the only one who has recognized this. Jonathan Chait, for example, has noted that "when Republicans [like Ryan] invoke the horrors of the national debt, they don't actually mean the national debt. They mean big government." This is why Ryan, and many like him, despite all the talk of the perils of deficits, refuse to deviate at all from the GOP's "anti-tax orthodoxy." In the end, "[t]hey are left arguing that the debt threatens to destroy American civilization, but they would rather leave it unaddressed than agree to even a dime of higher taxes."[124]

This seeming incongruity is inexplicable without reference to Ayn Rand and the Objectivist school of extreme Libertarian thought:

> "Ryan sees the coming fiscal crisis not as the gap between revenue and outlay but as the prophecy of <u>Atlas Shrugged</u> come to life — an overbearing government punishing the productive to aid the unproductive and precipitating a total collapse:

> When Ryan warns of the specter of collapse, he is not merely referring to the alarming gap between government outlays and receipts, as his admirers in the media assume. (Every policy change of the last decade that increased the deficit—the Bush tax cuts, the Medicare prescription-drug benefit, the wars in Afghanistan and Iraq—Ryan voted for.) He is also invoking Rand's almost theological certainty that when a government punishes the strong to reward the weak, it must invariably collapse. That is the crisis his Path to Prosperity seeks to avert."[125]

Congressman Ryan has long been a noted devotee of Ayn Rand. He has publicly stated that "[t]he reason I got involved in public service, by and large, if I had to credit one thinker, one person, it would be Ayn Rand."[126] Today, Rand's writings are required reading for everyone working in Ryan's office.[127]

This is troubling. Ayn Rand is essentially the L. Ron Hubbard of American conservatism. And Objectivism is its closest approximation of a political/ideological cult.[128]

Time and space do not permit an in-depth analysis of Rand's school of libertarian thought, Objectivism, and its various wrinkles and permutations. Thankfully, its essence has already been distilled for us by Charlie Sheen: "Winning!" It really all comes down to that. And from an Objectivist perspective, Winners have a special virtue, a superiority that differentiates them from everyone else. This gives Winners the right, no, more than that, the responsibility, to be selfish. The flip side of this is a tendency to see the poor as somehow lacking in virtue- they are poor because they are lazy, because they have defective or deficient characters, because they are just not quite smart enough to make the cut.

The only thing holding back the Winners from achieving even more is the rest of us, and especially the poor and the government that supports and protects them through social welfare programs. To an Objectivist, Winners are producers; the poor are a drain, an anchor holding society back... useless mouths. The greatest sin is to take from Winners and redistribute to the poor.

In the words on Jonathan Chait, "[t]he enduring heart of Rand's totalistic philosophy was Marxism flipped upside down. Rand viewed the capitalists, not the workers, as the producers of all wealth, and the workers, not the capitalists, as useless parasites."[129]

Understanding this is the key to grasping the intellectual and ethical coldness at the heart of much of modern libertarian thought, as well as its tendency towards Social Darwinism. It also explains the deep hostility of many radical libertarians towards the federal government, the entity that takes from Winners and places boundaries and restraints on their selfishness.[130]

Ryan's budget proposal is, in many ways, an Objectivist document. As Chait has noted, the "overwhelming thrust" of the proposal is a desire "to liberate the lucky and the successful to enjoy their good fortune without burdening them with any responsibility for the welfare of their fellow citizens."[131] As a result, Ryan's plan slashes spending on social programs that benefit the poor and the middle class while, simultaneously, reducing the tax burden on the wealthiest members of our society.[132] This is inexplicable from a policy standpoint, and indefensible from an ethical one. But it makes perfect sense if you see the world from an Objectivist perspective.

Ryan's proposals on Medicare have attracted the most attention. Essentially, he'd replace the current version with a voucher system for everyone presently aged 55 and younger in 2022 and beyond.[133] This may sound innocuous, but it has tremendous financial implications for individuals in the working and middle classes attempting to save for retirement. Given projected increases in healthcare costs, it is extremely unlikely that most of us will be able to purchase insurance comparable to today's Medicare post-2022.[134] In Ryan's vision, "prosperity" is apparently some sort of Orwellian new-speak for learning to live with a *lot less*.

But Ryan would also dramatically slash spending on a range of other social programs such as food stamps and the Special Supplemental Program for Women, Infants, and Children ("WIC").[135] He is proposing this at a time when many Americans are either unemployed, or under-employed. A time when one in seven of us (and one in five children) are on food stamps. And remember, food stamps and WIC are means-tested programs. How these people will eat is not explained in Ryan's proposal. Perhaps they will eat cake?

At the same time, Ryan's proposal would reduce taxes for the richest Americans, the Winners. Thus, the "Path to Prosperity" contains "a massive, regressive tax cut."[136] Specifically, Ryan would make the Bush tax cuts permanent while, simultaneously, reducing the top marginal personal income tax rate to 25%.[137]

Most Americans understand that entitlement reform is necessary. Many of us recognize that core social programs are on unsustainable trajectories. And we know that simply raising taxes, or eliminating tax exemptions, standing alone, isn't an answer. But I don't think Ryan's proposal is a reform- it's more like an Objectivist evisceration, both of the social contract, and of the power of the federal government itself.

As Pope Benedict XVI has taught in the encyclical *Caritas in Veritate*: "Many people today would claim that they owe nothing to anyone, except to themselves. They are concerned only with their rights, and they often have great difficulty in taking responsibility for their own and other people's integral development. Hence it is important to call for a renewed reflection on how rights presuppose duties, if they are not to become mere license." Sadly, the budgetary proposals of Congressional Republicans are a repudiation of the Pope's urgent call.[138]

In the midst of economic and fiscal crisis, it is important

that we not lose sight of our shared responsibilities for each other, and for our society as a whole. Now, more then ever, we need to attend to the commons, and to the common good. We need to ensure that our economy, and our government, equitably distributes the benefits and burdens generated by both booms and busts.

In the end, if you are in the middle or working classes, then Ryan's proposal isn't a "Path to Prosperity"- it is a roadmap to oligarchy and systemic inequality. It repudiates our obligation to the common good, and ignores our responsibilities towards the most vulnerable members of our society. And that's a path I'd rather not tread.

--

[123] Chait, Jonathan. (April 10, 2011). "War on the Weak." The Daily Beast.

[124] Chait, Jonathan. (May 2, 2011). "What Republicans Mean When They Say They Fear the Debt." The New Republic. Indeed, an anonymous Republican Congressional staffer told The Atlantic Monthly that Republicans are not being intellectually honest in the budget debate: "in the real world, fixing the deficit is a matter of national survival. When you get down to the real world decisions, it's not about whether to raise taxes. It's about the ratio of spending to revenue increases." See Thompson, Derek. (May 11, 2011). "GOP Aide: Republicans Not 'Intellectually Honest' on Taxes." The Atlantic Monthly. Retrieved from: http://www.theatlantic.com/politics/archive/2011/05/gop-aide-republicans-not-intellectually-honest-on-taxes/238756/

[125] Chait, "What Republicans Mean When They Say They Fear the Debt."

[126] Chait, "War on the Weak"

[127] Beam, Christopher. (Dec. 26, 2010). "The Trouble With Liberty." New York Magazine.

[128] See: Walker, Jeff. (1999). "The Ayn Rand Cult." (Peru, Illinois: Open Court Publishing Co.).

[129] Chait, "War on the Weak."

[130] And as Paul Nevis has cogently observed, today, the Randian glorification of selfishness "can only be endorsed as a panacea by those who are oblivious to the economic and political evidence from American history and contemporary events." Nevins, Paul. (April 19, 2011). "Ayn Rand and the Paradox of Selfishness." The Politics of Selfishness. Retrieved from: http://www.politicsofselfishness.com/2011/04/-ayn-rand-and-the-paradox-of-selfishness.html

[131] Chait, Jonathan. (Dec. 28, 2010). "Paul Ryan and Ayn Rand." The New Republic.

[132] Lux, Mike. (April 6, 2011). "The Cal Coolidge/Paul Ryan Budget." Crooks and Liars. Retrieved from: http://crooksandliars.com/taxonomy/term/4325,962,7872

[133] As Paul Krugman has observed, although Ryan's proposal ostensibly guarantees Americans over 55 today's version of Medicare, it creates an "unstable" and, in my opinion, unsustainable dynamic by creating two very different healthcare systems for senior citizens in the future- the lucky ones with the "old" version of Medicare, and the rest of us. See: Krugman, Paul. (April 5, 2011). "The 2022 Medicare Crisis." The New York Times.

[134] According to an analysis of the "Path to Prosperity" by the Congressional Budget Office, Ryan's proposal would actually increase healthcare costs overall, because private insurance is more expensive to purchase. See: Levey, Noam N. (April 7, 2011). "Rep. Paul Ryan's Medicare privatization plan increases costs, budget office says." Los Angeles Times.

[135] Byler, Eric. (May 12, 2011). "Analysis of 'Paul Ryan Budget' by National Priorities Project." CoffeePartyUSA. Retrieved from: http://www.coffeepartyusa.com/ryan-budget-npp

[136] Chait, Jonathan. (April 5, 2011). "The Achilles Heel Of The Path To Prosperity." The New Republic.

[137] Chait, Jonathan. (April 20, 2011). "Yes, Paul Ryan Does Cut Taxes For The Rich." The New Republic.

[138] Recognizing this, a group of Catholic clergy and professors have sharply criticized House Speaker Boehner (a Catholic) for his roll in passing a budget proposal that "guts long-established protections for the most vulnerable members of our society." See: Marrapodi, Eric. (May 11, 2011). "Catholic professors blast Boehner's record over cuts to poor." CNN. Retrieved from: http://religion.blogs.cnn.com/2011/05/11/catholic-professors-want-boehner-to-reconcider-cuts/?hpt=C2

19.

The Wisdom of Our Elders

December 10, 2011 will mark the 63rd Anniversary of the adoption of the Universal Declaration of Human Rights by the United Nations in 1948.[139]

The UN is not a popular body with many conservatives, and, frankly, much of the scourging it receives from the Right is amply justified. I am not speaking here of the fevered imaginings of conspiracy theorists, but rather, of very real scandals like Human Rights Commissions chaired by totalitarian regimes, such as Libya,[140] that make a mockery of the very concept of universal human rights. We can also point to the sordid spectacle of a General Assembly seemingly always at the ready to condemn Israel, while standing silent as terrible atrocities are perpetrated on other corners of the planet. To this short list might be added endemic corruption and sundry other woes.

Perhaps it was inevitable that the United Nations would

never live up to the high expectations of its founders. Collective defense, after all, was always destined to founder on the rocks of diverging national interests - as dangers and opportunities, benefits and burdens are never evenly distributed across the international system. Moreover, to paraphrase a famous quote, collective defense is unnecessary when unanimity exists about a threat, and essentially unworkable absent such a consensus.

Be that as it may, and despite the ample amounts of justly deserved criticism that can and should be leveled at the U.N., the Universal Declaration of Human Rights remains a document worth celebrating. Quite simply, it represents the collective wisdom of Western civilization on human rights as it emerged from the horrors of the Second World War.

We would do well to remember the dark passage of the war years - the global cataclysm - that set the context for the adoption of the Declaration, and to revisit its clear, unambiguous statement about the dignity of every person. Horror, after all, is not something confined to the history books. We flirt dangerously with a descent into new and more awful forms of barbarism the moment we forget that, in the words of the Declaration, the "recognition of the inherent dignity and of the equal and inalienable rights of all members of the human family is the foundation of freedom, justice and peace in the world." This principle has been, and remains, the sole basis upon which a more decent common future can be constructed.

In solidarity, then, with all those whose dignity and rights are denied, wherever they may be.

--

[139] United Nations. "The Universal Declaration of Human Rights." Retrieved from: http://www.un.org/en/documents/udhr/

[140] BBC News. (January 20, 2003). "Libya takes human rights roll." Retrieved from: http://news.bbc.co.uk/2/hi/africa/2672029.stm

20.
Lighting Up the Night: A Plea for Literacy

"And God said, 'Let there be light,' and there was light."-
Genesis 1:3

In the science fiction novel, *Fahrenheit 451*, Ray Bradbury depicts a future in which the state is so fearful of the power of ideas that it organizes massive book burnings of prohibited literature. As portrayed in the novel, these scenes call to mind the pyres constructed by the Nazi's and other totalitarians in our own time in their desperate attempts to erase and extinguish impermissible thoughts.

But the premise of Bradbury's dystopian future is flawed. As the author Chris Hedges has noted, there is no need to ban books or burn them in a world where no one wants to read.[141] Nor, is there any reason to fear the power of ideas if no one wants to think.

Sadly, we inhabit such a world today.

We live in a post-print world - one dominated by the functionally, or voluntarily, illiterate. For practical purposes, even many of the college educated today fall into the latter category. In our society, the written word has been replaced by the visual image. Today, most individuals derive their information from visual media - from pictures. That is problematic. Images can be easily manipulated, twisted, edited.[142] Also, visual imagery is not conducive to conveying complex or subtle ideas. The visual image generates a visceral, emotional impact. It conveys a literal world, one devoid of ambiguity or nuance. It is also, particularly in conjunction with the 24-hour news cycle, a world fixated on the present, providing little perspective on what came before, or of what may come after. It traps us in a prison of the moment, of the "now."

For these reasons, visual communication media are conducive to propaganda, and social control. Bradbury understood this. For example, in the novel, a character notes that the mechanical hound does not "think anything we don't want it to think." In one way, the mechanical hound serves as a metaphor for the people in the book. Like the hound, the characters' universe of thoughts and opinions is defined *for them*, not *by them*.

Today, in our era of mass, commercialized, popular culture, it often seems as if this aspect of Bradbury's vision has come to pass.

Unlike visual mediums, the written word is a window on the depth and complexity of the world around us. It allows us to think rationally, to reason. It is the key to knowledge. It exposes the hollowness of the ideological and theological dogmas and orthodoxies put forth by the extremists in our midst. Literacy is also the key to waking up from the dreamlike web of illusions spun around us by mass culture.

Literacy and learning are inseparable. Our culture once valued learning, the quest for knowledge, understanding, and enlightenment but does so no longer. The Founding Fathers, for example, were conversant in the Greek and Roman classics, as well as with the leading political theorists of their day. What politician reads Cicero or Locke today? Even more significantly, it wasn't just the Founders, the elite, participating in the dialogue about whether to break with England or, later, about how to structure our new Republic. Significant segments of the population were literate enough to join in, or at least, follow along. What newspaper or magazine, today, would publish works like the Federalist Papers? And what audience would there be to read them?

In former times, learning was seen as the path to happiness. But our culture today craves only entertainment, a word that is virtually synonymous with distraction and diversion.[143] The written word supports rational though in a way that visual images, standing alone, cannot. Today, our inability to follow language that is necessarily complex leads us to simple and superficial understandings and limits our ability to delve deeply into the complexity of the world and ideas. Thus, our post-literate world is, perforce, a shallow intellectual sea - one in which most people do not possess the vocabulary, the symbols, or the means to think critically or converse seriously about the problems facing our nation and the world. Instead, all we have are empty slogans.

Russell Kirk once wrote that those half and quarter educated, along with the bored, are the groups most to be feared in a democracy.[144] They are drawn to the false security and deceiving simplicity of the dogmas presented by the ideologues, of whatever political or theological stripe. In a way, political extremism and ignorance - about the world, about our history, about even ourselves - always travel in tandem.

If Kirk was right, then we are in terrible peril. Our capacity to reason, to learn, is the light in the void. It is time to "light up the darkness."[145] Together, we must develop a renewed cultural emphasis on learning- one that recognizes the value of knowledge and literacy.

--

[141] Hedges, Chris. (Dec. 27, 2010). "2011: A Brave New Dystopia." Truthdig.com. Retrieved from: http://www.truthdig.com/report/item/2011_a_brave_new_dystopia_20101227

[142] Ironically, the same is true, to a point, for many written works in the digital age. Thus, there is a need to distinguish between printed literature and newer electronic print media- the former is more fixed, the latter, far more mutable.

[143] Consider, for example, the French word for "entertainment"- divertissement.

[144] Kirk, R. (1993). The Politics of Prudence. (Wilmington, Del.: ISI Books), 7.

[145] This phrase appears at the conclusion of the film I Am Legend.

21.

God's Calling: Too Often, We Mistake the Sound of our own Egos for the Voice of God

Every election season, politicians publically claim, in one way or another, that they are somehow God's instrument. The speakers vary, but the general theme is always the same: God told them to run for office and their victory is somehow part of the great cosmic working out of His plan for humanity.

Now, to be clear, I believe in spiritual callings. And I also think God speaks directly to us and provides direction for us in our lives. But hearing politicians speak like this - well, it sounds both vain and inauthentic, doesn't it?

Frankly, I think too often we hear the sound of our own

egos, and mistake it for the voice of God.

When God speaks to you, He does not beckon you to fame and public acclaim or to an exulted position in society. Instead, He demands that you put aside your own selfish wants and desires and lead a life of humble service. Think about it - the deal offered the apostles didn't include status in their society. Nor did it include power or political influence. Instead, it literally was a call to cast aside their lives as they had known them, forget their own ambitions and dreams for the future, and instead lead lives of service to the Lord. That kind of call is terrifying, life-changing, transformative. Come to think of it, it was that other fellow that took Jesus up the mountain and spread before him all the kingdoms of the world, wasn't it?

And then there is Christ's messianic mission itself. It wasn't what the Jews expected. They were looking for a political and military messiah - one that would help them throw off the shackles of Roman domination. That isn't what they got and the contrast is telling. Christ's salvific mission didn't involve political or military glory, but rather humility, service and, ultimately, a self-sacrificial death. He spent His life with the poor and the most marginalized, not with leaders, rulers, or people of social or economic distinction.

Are we to believe, then, that today God's will is for people to rise to exalted positions of power and have their ambitions fulfilled? No, He calls us to be servants, to be humble and anonymous washers of feet; not to earthly glory playing at Herod or Caesar. The person who really, truly, hears His call is off working in a soup kitchen or volunteering at a hospice - not standing in front of a television camera. His path for us is always self-effacing. Public service can be a vocation, but only when the primary motivation for it is service to others and to the common good.

The prayer of the politician... the prayer of each of us, must be "Thy will be done Lord" - "*Thy*," not "*my*." The real trick then, of course, is to have the courage to heed the call, when His voice beckons and we are led "*where we do not wish to go*."[146]

Of one thing I am certain. When God calls you, it is never to send you off on an ego trip. To hear what He really wishes for us, we have only to quiet our own ambitions and desires.... and listen.

--

[146] John 21:18

22.
Are You Carrying the Fire?

"The Road" by Cormac McCarthy is a recent fictional work about a man and his son living ten years after what appears to be a major asteroid or comet strike (though the exact nature of the cataclysm is never defined) in a dystopian, post-apocalyptic future.

In their world, the sky is filled with ash. The sun is blotted out. Plants, animals, and most people are dead. Civilization has fallen apart and, with food stocks exhausted, many of the survivors have turned to cannibalism. The world is growing progressively colder and darker. In such circumstances, hope seems... irrational.

The characters decide to head south to the coast hoping it is warmer there and to see if they can find "the good guys" who are still "carrying the fire." In the face of terror and despair, they do not lose the last of their hope, nor their humanity.

The book is about love in the midst of crushing adversity, but it can also be viewed as a work of Christian allegory - religious themes and metaphors permeate the text. Indeed, the references to "carrying the fire" call to mind both Prometheus and the dawn of civilization as well as the imagery of Pentecost.

At a fundamental level, "The Road" speaks to the dilemma faced by people of good will in modernity. In an ethical, moral and cultural sense, we live in a blasted, darkening landscape that is growing progressively colder, where it is hard to find real sustenance - sustenance for the soul. We are surrounded by functional cannibals, who would live by (figuratively) destroying and devouring us. It is a world devoid of the sacred, one in which human dignity and solidarity, those bedrocks underpinning our humanity, are under constant assault. It is a place where human beings are commodified and reduced to the status of mere objects. The culture grows coarser, and we grow ever more brutalized. Unsurprisingly, it is marked by increasing hopelessness, anomie, and alienation. It is a world where the light of the Son is obscured.

The road is, in the end, the path of our lives in the modern world.

As individuals carrying the fire, we have limited power to effect the direction of the world. The full might of mass culture is turned against us, negating the good, mocking the truth, demeaning the quest for knowledge, promoting a set of values and norms at odds with authentic human development. It erects false idols and summons us to worship. And in those calls, it is as seductive as the Sirens. Even more than that, it creates a spectacle so distracting, and a realm of illusion so inviting, that men and women are not even sensible to their peril and, in many ways, are made the overseers of their own servitudes. Today, we often have no need for sadists to torment us, for we willingly degrade ourselves and serve as the instruments of our own debasement.

But, it is as pointless to curse the times as it is to curse the tides. Our duty in these perilous times is to carry the fire, to keep it lit, and to ensure that it is passed on to the next generation.

Stepping out onto the road is an act of bravery, of real moral courage. But, we are compelled to it because the fire cannot be kept alight in isolation, in a hermetic existence. It is a social thing. It requires community. And so we must venture forth and find each other in this world. In a way, all people of good will are on the road, trying to find the good guys, and struggling to keep the fire lit.

But, we face a dilemma. It is impossible to live in the modern world, to walk the road today, and not be morally compromised in some way. It is difficult to keep our bearings, and to retain the ability to distinguish good from bad, right from wrong. In such circumstances, how can we live ethical lives and maintain our own humanity?

The answer begins with human dignity - with the recognition that you are sacred, have intrinsic value, and that the "other" is your brother and is sacred and has intrinsic value too. The sacred isn't hidden from you, or hard to find - you encounter it every time you look into another's eyes.

So, on this road we travel, seize every opportunity to affirm our common humanity and demonstrate your love of your brothers and sisters. Expose cruelty and inhumanity wherever you find them. Be generous and compassionate. Do what you can for the weak, and the poor, and the most marginalized. Never lose sight of them. Cultivate that most angelic of emotions - empathy - so that, like Lear on the barren heath, you will be sensible to their sufferings and "expose thyself to feel what wretches feel."[147] For the ultimate negation of the doomsday Cult of Self is empathy - the ability to step beyond yourself and see from the perspective of another human being. Do not become complicit in the debasement or degradation of another. Take no pleasure in such spectacles. Be a good steward of creation, and tend life's common spaces. Learn to see through the images, the illusions, to the substance of things.

If we do these things, then the insatiable Moloch will never devour us, nor will we lose ourselves in its gaping maw. If we do these things, then the truth will never be shorn of its referents in the world. If we do these things together, then we will preserve our own integrity and keep the fire burning, until better days.

And the fire will warm our souls on this journey - reminding us that life has a purpose and meaning that transcends mere survival.

Perfer et obdura - endure and persevere.

I'll see you on the road.

--

[147] Shakespeare, William, King Lear, Act 3, Scene IV

###

About the author

Michael Stafford graduated magna cum laude from Washington College in Chestertown, Maryland, where he received the Louis L. Goldstein '35 Award, given annually to a "graduating senior who demonstrates an unusual interest, enthusiasm, and potential in the field of public affairs." He went on to earn his Juris Doctorate from Duke University School of Law. He practices law in Wilmington, Delaware.

Politically, Mr. Stafford formerly served on both the Delaware State Republican Committee and on the New Castle County Republican Committee, where he chaired its Transportation Working Group. He remains active in politics as the Delaware Coordinator for Republicans for Environmental Protection.

Mr. Stafford has been a guest on CoffeePartyUSA's internet radio program and has spoken at numerous local, regional, and national conferences and seminars including the Ragan Communications "Corporate Communicators Conference." His writing has appeared on a number of local and national blogs including FrumForum, CoffeePartyUSA, Moonhowlings, Resolute Determination, and TommyWonk, as well as in The Dialog (the newspaper for the Catholic Diocese of Wilmington, Delaware). Mr. Stafford is also a regular contributor to Town Square Delaware.

Mr. Stafford can be reached via email at
AnUpwardCalling@yahoo.com.